PRAISE FOR THE ART OF THE REAL

"A fast-paced creative business memoir from a truly authentic voice, *The Art of the Real* tells the story of a kid from a New York immigrant family who became a real estate mogul by seeking creative investments. Lebensohn's story shows how embracing a win-win mindset and emphasizing relationships above everything else is the true road to success."

JOE POLISH, FOUNDER OF THE GENIUS NETWORK AND GENIUS RECOVERY

"Daniel Lebensohn writes thoughtfully and from the heart. His business and life insights always compel deeper conversation so having him share empirical reflections with the rest of us in *The Art of the Real* is a true gift."

SIMON ZIFF, PRESIDENT AND CO-FOUNDER OF THE ACKMAN-ZIFF REAL ESTATE GROUP

"*The Art of the Real* is a book to be read over and over. Daniel Lebensohn is a visionary, a philosopher and an artist."

DAVID PAUL KAY, CONTEMPORARY
ARTIST

"Powerful, real and extraordinary like the man himself. *The Art of the Real* is a must-read book for all visionaries and dreamers!"

DOMINGO ZAPATA, SPANISH ARTIST,
WRITER AND FASHION DESIGNER

THE
ART
DANIEL N. LEBENSOHN

OF THE
REAL LIFE
REAL RELATIONSHIPS
AND REAL ESTATE

REAL

DISCLAIMER

This work is non-fiction and, as such, reflects the author's memory of the experiences. Many of the names and identifying characteristics of the individuals featured in this book have been changed to protect their privacy, and certain individuals are composites. Dialogue and events have been recreated; in some cases, conversations were edited to convey their substance rather than written exactly as they occurred.

To Tamir and Zohar—you are my everything.

CONTENTS

INTRODUCTION

In 2003, I recall sitting on the balcony on Williams Island in Miami, specifically to get away from the noise of the Charlie Brown-like banter taking place inside the apartment. The balcony had a view of Dumfoundling Bay and the islands floating in it, one north and one south. I had yet to have any meaningful real estate deals under my belt and was still grinding it out in the practice of law. I was drinking a beer and daydreaming as I watched construction crews move around the South Island. I knew through the Aventura grapevine and gossip mill that the South Island was being developed by a guy named Gary Cohen, a well-established real estate developer in the area who was building luxury residential homes there—but it puzzled me that the North Island wasn't being developed. The North Island was a hidden gem in the middle of a densely developed area, one with so much creative and financial potential that it made my imagination spin. Whoever earned the privilege of developing it would be the luckiest team in the world; it would be the project of a lifetime. It never occurred to me that the people to develop it would be my partners and me.

Ten years later, I was crossing the bridge from the South Island to the North with Gary Cohen and Greg Freedman, my business partner at BH3 Management. Gary unlocked a chain bolted fence, and we walked out onto the island—a completely blank canvas. I was in awe! How was this possible?

After years of buying distressed debt, fixing busted projects and flipping real estate assets that other investors would not touch, it felt like a mirage. The comedy of it was that this was to be our first as-of-right-entitled project. Unlike our prior acquisitions, this was not a property that needed repairs or financial restructuring or that was riddled with legal issues. Because I see everything through the eyes of a New Yorker, I couldn't help but think it was like walking down Park Avenue and finding an open green swath with a sheepherder and his flock in the middle of it, surrounded by high rises. It was quiet, flat land in the middle of the bay, ripe for us to create something extraordinary.

I turned to look at the adjacent peninsula known as Williams Island, where I had once sat on that balcony looking down, and considered how far I'd come. Gary Cohen had once seemed a reclusive titan of industry; now he was becoming a close friend. Greg had started as merely a business colleague, but I'd come to know him as an old soul, a brilliant mind and a brother—but it had taken a broader team of close friends and business peers investing with us and offering their wisdom to bring our project to fruition.

There was Ari Goldman, who advocated for us, opened doors and made crucial introductions; Harry Zubli and Scott

Hurwitz offered sharp legal insights and went toe-to-toe with huge law firms; Greg Freedman was an incredible friend and a wizard of financial engineering; Kurt Jacobs invested, consulted and offered support. They were all lifelong friends I'd known from growing up in Long Island and later practicing law in New York City, but now they were coming together like a team of legal and financial superheroes to make the impossible happen. The power of those relationships had connected dots and created opportunities I'd never thought possible. Now, we were holding all the brushes and could simply paint. (Not 30 days later, we were hit with a lawsuit, but that story will be revealed in time).

Before I entered the world of real estate, I dreamed of being a writer. Although that dream did not materialize (until now), my artistic temperament has been with me my entire life. In developing major commercial and residential buildings, it has always been my tendency to romanticize and imagine my buildings are alive—in the energy and community the tenants bring to them, in the art and culture that artists and muralists contribute and in the histories of the actual structures themselves.

The garages and basements of my buildings are my favorite places to think; as I do so, I breathe in the energy of the structure and all its inhabitants. It is an ideal way to feel for a building's pulse. All my supers know that I insist upon those hidden spaces being kept immaculately clean, with all the pipes correctly color-coded; bright red for hot and blue for cold water lines, no matter how old the building—because the pipes are the arteries and veins bringing lifeblood to every family in each unit.

This may seem like an unusual way to start a book of

reflections about a life in real estate, but I have no intention of drafting yet another "how-to" or "how-not-to" treatise. There is certainly no shortage of advice on how to be successful and live the good life today, although what that means depends on who you ask.

We have become accustomed to seeing people showcasing the methods and results of their success (assuming their "results" are as genuine as they seem), but we don't often get to access the mind and soul behind it all. Big successes can emerge spontaneously out of difficult situations, but often, they are built on prior successes. With that in mind, the mere fact of a person's financial success is an insufficient indicator to those appraising it. How can we know if there is any actual substance behind the inflated bank statements (and the even more inflated egos)? What if the person behind a project is just repackaging what others have created before them? Other than money, do they have any skin in the game? Are they really telling a true story others can learn from, or are they sugarcoating it?

We get a lot of the *what* and some of the *how*, but few people talk about the *why*. As an artistic soul who has succeeded in business, I hope to convey to aspiring entrepreneurs that art and business need not be separate—in fact, they shouldn't be. From my perspective, *everything* is art. Life is a blank canvas, and the major brushstrokes you put on it are your relationships, with all the color and texture found in the stories behind each one. They may not seem so significant taken individually, but when one retreats to see the big picture, a beautiful, interconnected fabric of color emerges. It is all that connectivity and beauty that makes up your life's journey, and it is out of those relationships that material success and deeper fulfillment emerge.

Making and closing business deals has been a lifelong pursuit of mine. I have been doing it since I was just a kid and have always genuinely loved it. After gaining years of experience as a lawyer and real estate investor, my business partner Greg and I created a thriving, multimillion-dollar real estate business called BH3 Management. Our portfolio over the years has consisted of properties throughout Florida and New York, many of which are high-rise residential units and luxury condominium complexes.

We have transacted more than $1.5 billion in investment deals and have delivered outsized returns to our investors and partners. Our business endeavors have employed hundreds of people, and our properties have impacted many diverse communities. Many of our renovations have started bold conversations, particularly as a result of the artistic touches we bring to our properties. I attribute our success not to my own individual abilities or achievements but to the strength of the relationships undergirding them. My childhood friends are still by my side, and our combined imaginative powers have together created thriving business ventures and lifelong bonds. Those relationships have provided all the color of my life; they are the magic that makes everything possible. But that's the upside.

It's only right that I also share the downside.

In the interest of full transparency, I will tell you that my adult entrepreneurial journey started with massive failure. I have worked dozens of different jobs: some of them I quit; others were offers revoked at the last second. After working a traditional law job after graduation, I launched an online start-up for real estate auctions. Though my company had no competitors and was primed to tap into the World Wide Web, a geographically limitless market with endless prospects, I ultimately lost every penny I had when the dot-com bubble burst. I had to pick myself up, let go of the negativity attached to the failure, recover my pride and identify a brand-new path towards my goals. The road I followed was far from smooth, and challenges continue to present themselves to this very day. While writing this, I have been fighting through serious brain fog from a recent concussion sustained from flipping my bike while riding on the Appalachian Trail. My family and I are in the middle of a painful and lengthy divorce process, one that has burned up invaluable time and energy, created unwelcome distraction and depleted many valuable resources.

For nearly a full decade of my life, I felt like I was drifting further from my dreams and inching closer to the dreaded 9-5 work mill grind. I started several businesses and side hustles before BH3, nearly all of which floundered due to a lack of genuine interest and motivation. Because of those early endeavors, my practice now is to take dozens of meetings on hundreds of properties and potential investments for everyone BH3 ultimately chooses to pursue. The success of a project is directly linked to the care with which it was initially identified and selected, and so the work begins before the project is even ours.

Most people don't want to hear this, which is why it's important to say it at the starting line: the realization of a fulfilling life, the one you picture in your wildest dreams, is really fucking hard. So is building and running a successful business. The process of finding good investments, developing strong relationships and earning a positive reputation can be grueling and thankless. At BH3, my partner and I have a running joke premised on this reality: "This is the deal that's going to put us on the map!" The details of the deal do not matter; the map can always expand, so the joke is always relevant. When we don't have all the money and status we fantasize about, we imagine that getting those things will solve all our problems. We think that as our life becomes more convenient, we'll be more fulfilled. I'm entering the conversation to shut down that way of thinking.

The surface-level assets we have been taught to aspire to are, at best, symbols of success and accomplishment. But at worst, they are the raw materials for what I call "the money trap," an empty existence that is more outward illusion than spiritual substance. The truth is that the greatest rewards and the most fulfillment we can hope to have in life come through the meaningful connections we have with other people.

I'm not here to be Pollyanna, to denigrate the value of making money, or to say that hard work and sacrifice aren't important. I'm a big believer in paying your dues and taking responsibility for yourself. What I am saying is that all those things are valuable *because* they help you build good relationships—which in turn help you build good environments, good businesses and a better world. Sweat equity, as I like to call it, is usually not solely the result of one man's toil. Indisputably, work and its results are optimally rewarding when they are accomplished with others. By collaborating, you create something even bigger than just the thing that was built; you also forge irreplaceable bonds that overshadow the creation. From a financial perspective, the most beautiful

ROSEs—Returns On Sweat Equity—are grown by teaming up and combining everyone's creative power at once.

These are just some of the unexpected rewards of collaborative creation through relationships. The happiness that may elude us in life when we chase it directly appears naturally through the confluence of all that goodness. It is a second-order effect on the long path to fulfillment.

Just as our life canvas is woven of many individual strands to create a vibrant tapestry, in my vision of the ideal professional world, every business deal and venture becomes part of a complicated and intricate fabric. Each deal contains elements of all the people who came together to make it and all the unique backgrounds and perspectives they brought to bear on it. Of course, it's up to the specific individuals to move that theoretical ball of energy in a given direction—it can be dissolved for individual gain or pushed in the direction of expanding opportunities and enhancing the world at large.

Each situation presents its own judgment calls, but a word to the wise: repeatedly pursuing individual gain leads to burning bridges, tightening your circle and making the world around you smaller. By contrast, being open-hearted and creating opportunities for others leads to limitless possibilities, both on immediate projects and projects you have not yet even considered. You don't have to believe in karma to understand that the way you treat others has ripple effects that cause intergenerational impacts. Your success will either be a testament to the power of the strong relationships in your life or evidence that your lack of strong relationships is causing you to stagnate. When harnessed correctly, the power of solid relationships generates compounding growth effects that dwarf any other force I am aware of.

In real estate projects today, my team always teases out the creative touches we can bring to our projects and the FUN—Fascinating and Unique Nuances—each project offers beyond the potential cash returns. To me, real estate, relationships and life choices are all in the same category. They are all art to me, and to create a masterpiece, one needs to source both light and dark colors.

This book is for entrepreneurs of all stripes, whether newbies or billionaires, who want to bring their artistry and creativity back—not only to their businesses but also to their relationships and their lives. In any major venture, it is easy to get trapped in the mindset of chasing a dollar rather than using that dollar to build a life around what truly matters. This is a trap I have fallen into myself at times, and I would like to help as many people avoid it as possible.

It takes real dedication to build strong relationships, become financially successful, find fulfillment and produce the best outcomes for everyone along the way. It is a lot to keep in balance, and I don't claim to have all the answers; I simply offer my story. Take from it what you will.

1

THE IMMIGRANT MINDSET

> *"Everything can be taken from a man but one thing: the last of the human freedoms—to choose one's attitude in any given set of circumstances, to choose one's own way."*
> *-Viktor Frankl*

"Come on," my dad said to my sister and me when I was 10 years old. "I'll buy us all some ice cream." I was shocked.

My dad was a proud Jew from Vienna, Austria, who spent his formative years evading concentration camps and the Nazi war machine. As an immigrant who had become a highly regarded mathematician, spent 45 years as a professor commander at the United States Merchant Marine Academy and owned multiple rental properties, he still bought a used Dodge Dart from my friend Kurt Jacobs' grandmother after she'd already run it into the ground (and still sold it for profit years later). His first date with my mom —a fellow first-generation immigrant from Israel—was at the world-famous Junior's Deli in Brooklyn, and he was very impressed when all she ordered was a bowl of soup (though she jokes now that if she'd known they would spend the rest of their lives together, she would've ordered a sandwich too).

Because of my parents' provenance, growing up in our household felt more like being in Europe than American suburbia. We lived in a predominantly Jewish community of immigrants, each one more successful than the last and all of them entrepreneurial hustlers. It meant that in our house, nothing was wasted, almost everything was saved and anything purchased was usually purchased used—and if we ever bought something new, there was certain to be a long-winded drama leading up to it. If my sister and I ever wanted something, we would have to backchannel it to my mother, who then went about navigating an approval from my father, the ever-vigilant keeper of the purse strings.

Fortunately, my mother was resilient, unrelenting and downright creative as a negotiator; still, my father was also deeply resilient in an almost unhuman, superhero-like way. No amount of requests or diligent pursuit could move him; with every new effort to get to a "yes" on buying a new prod-uct, he would get stronger, like Popeye eating another can of spinach. Every time was like a hostage negotiation. To diffuse the tension, I took it upon myself to inject humor into our home with regular, healthy doses of sarcasm—like imitating him sitting in our cold kitchen refusing to put the heat up, insisting that he would put a jacket on instead and denying that it was cold at all (even as his neck was bright red and he was nearly shivering). Watching all of these exchanges taught me a simple lesson from a young age: to get the things you wanted, you had to fight for them.

One of the few times I remember going out to eat as a kid was when my father paid off the mortgage to our family home and took us to Peter Luger Steak House on Northern Boulevard in Long Island. The meal was exquisite—huge cuts of meat, steaming greens, massive bowls of mashed potatoes—but all my dad could comment on was the waiter's obsequious "dog and pony show." That dinner is singed into my brain because 20 years later, I still haven't heard the end of how "not worth it" it was.

To put it simply, impromptu ice cream trips were unheard of for my father—so my sister Alisa and I were more than eager to take advantage of his generosity.

We piled in the back of one of his many jalopies, this one a shit-brown Oldsmobile Cutlass sedan, and drove down Middle Neck Road to Carvel, an ice cream shop that was a local institution in our immigrant town of Great Neck, New York.

"What's going on?" my dad asked the upset-looking manager when we walked in. My dad was a master of sincere engagement and invariably struck up friendly conversations with workers in local shops wherever we went.

"We just got a huge delivery of product, and it's all worthless," the manager said with a frown. "I took the pallet out to check it out, and all the ice cream is crushed."

"Can I take a look at it?" my father asked.

The manager nodded, and the three of us followed him to the back of the big, white, freezer-filled ice cream parlor. As we gazed at the freezers, we noticed one of them had a cracked lid. Inside were a bunch of pre-packaged ice cream products—bonnets, flying saucers, cups, the works. It was all still frozen, but the packaging was beat up, and everything was misshapen.

"I can't sell this stuff to customers," the manager said.

The gears were turning in my dad's head. *It's still in the packaging*, I could practically hear him thinking. *What's the difference? It just needs to taste good and melt in my mouth. It all ends up in the same place: my stomach!* The product may have been no good by Carvel's glossy, corporate standards, but it was perfectly fine by our family's. Finally, my father spoke up. "Will you sell all of this to me?" he asked.

With barely any negotiation, we walked out of that store with an industrial-sized freezer of ice cream for pennies on the dollar, and my impressionable little mind was blown. My father paid the guy maybe $13 for the entire inventory! My mouth was already watering, thinking of all the ice cream my sister, my friends and I would stuff our faces with that summer. It was more ice cream than any sane private citizen should have room for in their home, but the basement of our house was like a Home Depot for used shit. There were two or three extra refrigerators sitting down there that my dad had bought throughout the years, having scooped them up for practically nothing at garage sales because they had had cosmetic defects—maybe one of the light bulbs didn't work, or maybe they were just old as hell. My mother used them during the holidays to store all her cooking pregame, but aside from that, all they did was collect dust.

When we got home that day, we plugged in the fridges, cleaned them off and filled them with glorious ice cream. My dad grinned. This was the latest in a long line of fixer-upper projects and questionable investments, and it had paid off big time. We would be eating Carvel ice cream for a year.

That moment left an indelible mark on me. It was a seed of knowledge about what I wanted to do with my life. My dad's contrarian thinking reminded me of how I felt at school when I had to sit in one place for too long. My father was a quiet and somewhat mysterious man. The deal he'd done had been impressive, but more significant was that for the first time, I could see him reflected in myself.

Inadvertently, he had given me permission to question authority in my own way, nurture my appetites and embrace what was unique about me. I could glimpse what I would do with my life: I would follow in my dad's footsteps by following my own path and challenging conventional thinking. It was one of the first times I dreamed of becoming a great entrepreneur (hopefully an even better one than my dad).

Ice cream windfalls aside, my father had modeled the millionaire-next-door mentality for as long as I could remember, and to some extent, so had many fathers in our community. My best friend Ari Goldman's dad had transitioned from growing up on a farm in Poland to building a successful multi-state retail business called C.H. Martin. My friend David Zarabi's dad started as a busboy when he first immigrated from Khomeini-controlled Iran in the 1980s, arriving in America with no money and zero command of the English language. He later became a successful real estate developer.

Most of my friends' dads had similar success stories, but of all of them, my dad may have been the most thoughtful and strategic about making his business ventures work for his particular lifestyle. Even before I was born, he was already leveraging his salary into his own modest real estate empire.

Before I was born, Dad bought his first house in 1963, which, to this day, he still owns and rents out as an investment property. He bought a second house in 1971, just one month before I was born. This one had been part of a large old estate on Long Island, which was subdivided into multiple single residence homes in a charming cul de sac in the town's old village and which ultimately became our family home. Around the same time as the Carvel ice cream incident, Dad bought a third house. This one looked like a chicken coop and was situated on a large, grassy plot of land deeply offset from the main road; it granted our tenant a privacy he cherished, though others might have viewed the house's distance from the access road as a nuisance. It was steps from a nature trail and cost a paltry $38,000, but it was how my dad gave me my first real taste of the real estate business.

Dad conducted his business over our kitchen table, where tenants would have meetings and sign their leases with me watching over their shoulders. Sometimes I would drive across town with my dad to fix a broken toilet or clogged sink, but most exciting of all was when he would take me across state lines with him to scout out potential new investments. After seeing his moxie firsthand, I didn't have to be told to get a job (and was never led to believe that having "a job" was the point at all). If I wanted to be a successful entrepreneur, I knew I had to get in the game right away.

I started packaging Penny Savers when I was about 12. An old van would pull in front of our house once a week to drop off reams of cheap newspaper that needed collating, and for about a year, I'd sit on the creaky floorboards of our family home on the weekends with an ocean of coupons littered around me. Once the papers were assembled, I threw them in a "borrowed" supermarket cart and rolled it around a half dozen blocks in my neighborhood, tossing papers onto my neighbors' doorsteps. It paid okay at the time, but I hadn't yet cracked my dad's code of working less, collecting passive income and doing what you wanted in your spare time. It took a couple of years of shoveling snow in the winters before I got fed up with the odd jobs.

Winters on Long Island were brutally cold, and the summers were scorching, which meant that all my neighbors' blacktops would regularly crack up and require repairs or replacement. As a result, my neighborhood was full of opportunities every summer for upstart landscapers and blacktoppers.

"Have you seen all those work crews driving around?" I asked Kurt one day when I was about 16.

"Yeah, who hasn't?"

"Why couldn't we do that ourselves?" I asked.

It certainly sounded more fun and lucrative than working another low-paying job. We would own our own business, get some exercise and make money in the process. We had just gotten our drivers' licenses, but truthfully, we'd been driving for years—it was a near-weekly habit of mine to wait until my parents were asleep and "borrow" their car for joyrides around Great Neck.

Kurt, David and I had spent many nights zooming around town blasting music, hanging out the windows and yelling like maniacs—so many that when Kurt took his driving test, his mother was baffled that he'd passed so flaw-lessly when she'd barely even taken him out to practice.

Still, we had no car to use for our business. Fortunately, I knew someone who did. "Dad, please," I asked him one day while he was trying to eat a sandwich in peace. "Kurt and I already have a business plan and a name picked out. We're calling ourselves 'The Private Corporation' or 'PC 1 Driveway Sealers,' and we're covering all the materials and advertising costs ourselves. We just need a way to get around. We'll take great care of any car you lend us, I promise."

He chewed slowly while thinking it over. My father didn't buy for a minute that Kurt and I would be careful while tearing around town in one of his cars with buckets of tar and gravel, but he also didn't care all that much. Material goods were never his main concern, which, in this case, worked in our favor. Dad knew that I was now putting all my energies into making money, which was far better than everything else I had been doing up to that point—namely staying out late, hanging out in Manhattan, scrapping with kids from Great Neck South (we went to Great Neck North) and not applying myself at school. All things considered, maybe a little extra wear and tear on one of his cars was worth it? Sure enough, he gave us the keys to a beat-up blue Datsun 510 mini wagon he'd been tinkering with, and we were off.

After slapping some logo stickers on the Datsun, knocking doors and passing out enough fliers to steal some business from bigger blacktopping companies in the area, Kurt and I drove to Home Depot to pick up tools and materi-als. We had to wake up as early as possible to stay out of the heat and avoid sunburns, and often, it meant that Kurt was knocking my door down at 5 am after I'd been out too late in the city the night before.

"Lebensohn, wake the hell up!" he'd yell, hammering on the door. Straight-A student that he was, Kurt was as disciplined about our business as he was about everything else in life, which made him a perfect business partner. We had connected in school because, in a lot of ways, we felt similarly situated. Compared to the rest of Great Neck (the wealthiest zip code in the country at the time, I believe), our families weren't rich; as a result, we both felt like outsiders. We knew that we'd have to hustle and scrap to get what we wanted. We'd also been working out together for years at the Merchant Marine Academy gym, so Kurt was no slouch when it came to the actual work of blacktopping—which turned out to be backbreaking after a while.

After just a few weeks, Kurt and I perpetually stunk like sweat and tar, and the Datsun had more scuffs and stains than when we had started. Still, we made between $300 and $600 per job, and we crammed in so many jobs that before long, we were making more than $1,200 to $2,000 a week! Not bad for a couple of high school kids. That first summer, we did most of the work ourselves and raked in a ton of cash, but we were already brainstorming about ways to offload the labor and keep more of the profits. The answer was simple enough: we recruited a handful of USMMA underclassmen to do the work for us while we focused on sales and lining up new work orders. By our second year in business—our senior year in high school—our business and profits were supercharged for less work than before, and the Datsun was freed up again for extracurricular activities.

One of my more productive activities was Video Abstracts, a business David and I started together filming real estate listings. Seeing our fathers' success, David, Ari and I were always talking about getting into real estate as soon as we could—and even if Video Abstracts didn't end up going anywhere, it was still good experience. Less productive were the joyrides we would go on in my 1978 Oldsmobile Cutlass Supreme.

I would pick up David from his house where his older brother Mikey, who was six years older than us and smoked cigarettes, would often be outside modding his 1987 Mustang 5.0. In my eyes, Mikey was like a Persian James Dean—always rebelling against the tight cultural and communal expectations of his Iranian community.

David and I had a favorite pastime of using my car to get into trouble. On one occasion, we were chasing a younger kid than us on a moped until he drove up a one-way the wrong way. I was hesitating about following him until David spoke up. "It's only illegal if you get caught!" he said with a smile. With him egging me on in the passenger seat, I revved the engine and sped down the road the wrong way, and not eight seconds later, we were pulled over by a cop.

Another day after shooting the shit with Mikey, David and I got in my car and started fishtailing it down local dirt roads. It was raining, and I lost control of the car, over-shooting the steering and slamming David's side of the car into a tree. We were fortunate that nobody was hurt, but the car was badly beat up. I drove home and made up some bull-shit excuse about what had happened with David stifling his laughter beside me.

"A dog jumped into the middle of the road, Dad!" I said. "There was nothing I could do."

"I don't care," my dad replied. "I'm not spending any money to repair it. You're going to drive it just the way it is." It meant that any time I picked up a date in my car after that, I sat slightly higher in the air, and she leaned into the door as far from me as possible because my entire car had a tilt. It was so noticeable that it was fondly referred to by a few friends at school as the old "Out of Whack."

With high school nearing its end, I felt like I was starting to outgrow Great Neck. I'd never applied myself much in school, except for in subjects I loved like math, business and shop class. I considered myself a survivor of the educational system more than a graduate. All the extra money I was making meant more to spend sneaking into clubs in New York City, taking girls out to fancy restaurants and chipping in on kegs for house parties with my friends—but one can only hit repeat on the proverbial jukebox for so long before the song starts to grate on one's nerves. Partying was fun, but I knew there was more that my life was meant to be. Running the blacktop business had allowed me to sample a life I actually wanted. Meanwhile, all my dad could talk about was the value of a college degree.

"Where are you thinking about school?" he would ask casually whenever we were in the same room. "Any thoughts about what you might study?" I told him again and again that I wanted to start a business, to keep making money the way I was and then get into real estate, just like him.

"It's not a bad idea, Daniel," he'd say, "but what's your plan? You need a means to your ends. Why not get your degree, establish yourself, make a little money and learn about real estate on the way?"

I wanted to jump into life headfirst. I was exploding with energy and ready to put it towards something I actually cared about. Still, my dad had made some valid points, and he was insistent. My compromise was that I would lazily apply to one school: Baruch College, City College of New York. My father had gone to Baruch himself, so he was satisfied ("It's the poor man's Harvard," according to him). Sure enough, I got in.

Even though I was still living at home, what appealed to me about Baruch was that it was in the city, something I'd already experienced more of than my parents likely knew. When the academic year commenced, I was driving to Manhattan every day to take classes (and getting in my fair share of chess at the tables in Washington Square Park between them). Still, I was mentally stuck in Great Neck. After classes, I was involved in an endless cycle of the same activities: going to parties, meeting girls, driving around town aimlessly and spending some of the money I'd worked hard to save. By the end of my first year of college, I was bored— and my parents weren't particularly impressed with my academic efforts.

To change my environment and sharpen my focus, I transferred to SUNY Albany sophomore year. I naturally settled on a business major and joined the Alpha Epsilon Pi fraternity. While the parties were the most visible outward element, I formed a lot of deep relationships and bonds that were a breath of fresh air.

I pledged with a guy named David Goldin, who had a twisted Larry David-esque perspective on things that never ceased to crack me up. He was determined to take action in nearly every situation and could be impatient in the process. One night, I was gearing up for an all-night writing session for a paper I had due the next morning when he came knocking at my door.

"Daniel, let's go out," he said. "I want to get some wings and meet up with some of those AEPhi girls."

"I can't go; I have to crank out this paper," I replied. "I'm going to be here all night." David moved quickly across the room and ushered me out of my chair, sitting in front of my laptop himself.

"Start talking, and I'll type," he said. Sure enough, and two hours later, *voila*, we had a good, finished paper (good enough for a C or better, at least). With that, we were off to eat 10-cent wings at the Lamp Post and meet girls. Though we both had our priorities in line, neither of us was ever meant to be in the standardized school system, which was part of why we bonded and became dear friends. While we may have been lazy students, we were relentless for things we were passionate about, like deconstructing businesses to figure out where opportunities lay hidden. We both had explosive, volcanic energy, and neither of us was built for convention.

Though I cherished the bonds I'd made with David and other fraternity brothers, I was falling into what amounted to a variation of the high school life I had long known; partying, getting in trouble, and flirting with beautiful sorority girls at mixers (sometimes more than flirting, if we're being honest). While some of my business courses were interesting, I still craved exposure to a bigger world—for real this time.

Because I'd been trying a little harder than usual at

Baruch compared to high school, my grades were reasonable. I looked at some study abroad programs and decided to try going to school in Israel at the Hebrew University in Jerusalem for a year. Once again, I was fortunate enough to get in.

My world in Long Island was relatively small, and virtually everyone I knew there was first-generation American, stemming from a wave of immigrant parents. We all had the scrappy, immigrant mindset that we needed to hustle to prove ourselves. Once in Jerusalem, I was captivated by how ancient and diverse the city felt.

Jerusalem was a thriving and well-established city with a million stories hidden in every street corner. There were exchange students at Hebrew University from all over the world. In my dorm, I had friends from France, Russia, Germany, Israel and the Middle East, and they would all regularly get into heated debates about life, world politics, art and literature. The dorms were sometimes the staging ground for Arab protestors, many of whom were friends I sat, drank tea and exchanged ideas with in the most respectful and peaceful way. Every night, my bedroom turned into a philosophical salon. One evening, a Russian friend of mine named Eliyahu brought two Parisiennes, Dora and Sylvia, to my dorm and set about trying to impress them.

"Have you read *Crime and Punishment*?" Eliyahu asked them as he poured glasses of wine. Instantly, they both lit up.

"Oui!" Dora replied warmly, taking her glass.

"Was Raskolnikov justified in killing Alyona Ivanova?"

"She deserved it!" Sylvia shouted. "She exploits the poor; she enslaves her sister—"

"Yes, but isn't the point that the murder can't be justified? Even on moral grounds?" They were speaking perfect English, but they may as well have been speaking Russian and French. In Long Island, I'd been interested in girls, money and getting into local squabbles. Until the age of about 19, I'd mainly read for necessity (for school assignments or at gunpoint). I'd never read much about life, art or philosophy, so all I could do was smile and nod because I hadn't read the book. I was totally left out.

I got the lesson loud and clear: to be a part of the conversation, you had to do the reading. I planned to be part of the conversation—maybe even to lead it one day.

The next morning, I went to an open book market and found a used copy of *Crime and Punishment*. I cracked it open that same day and was surprised to find myself entirely absorbed, skipping courses for three days to finish it in as close to one sitting as possible. This was nothing like the books I'd been forced to read in high school! The psychology was complex and tortured, and the characters were dealing with profound struggles. It wasn't just about a tenant named Raskolnikov who murdered his landlord and tried to escape a detective—it was about the nature of justice, about God, about human guilt and the responsibilities we have to one another. I holed up in my dorm room for three days devouring that book, and when it was over, I wanted more. Before long, my concerns about money and girls were fading into the background. I wanted to experience all the depth life had to offer.

After that first semester, Hebrew University went on winter break. It was the first time in 40 years there had been snowfall in Jerusalem—and ironically enough, given my new favorite book, Israel had just welcomed many Russian refugees (the joke in the streets that winter was that God had made the snow to make them feel more at home). Over the break, I took a six-week trip that started with a dumpy ship ride to the Port of Piraeus in Athens. It felt like the first great adventure of my life, and it seemed like a good idea to stick with some of the other Americans I'd met to get my bearings. As it turned out, I was wrong.

"Let's go to the bar and get wasted!" they would shout after setting foot in every new port town we stopped in. I was getting flashbacks to Albany and Great Neck. I could already see the cycle ahead: every day we would get up late, spend money getting blasted, sleep in until noon the next day and repeat.

"Guys," I told them, "I love you all, and I want you to have an extraordinary time. But respectfully, I think we have to go our separate ways." That was good enough for them; they were off to the dives, and I was ready to break out on my own. With just my backpack, my ID, some cash and a little credit, I explored the Greek Islands, Turkey, France and Amsterdam with nothing tying me down or holding me back. I absorbed beautiful architecture, met fascinating people and tried to absorb snippets of local languages. I discovered that any tourists who mastered even a handful of phrases in the native tongue got doors opened for them that might have otherwise remained closed. The experience was bringing something new out of me that I didn't recognize, but I liked it.

When I returned to Jerusalem after the break, I was hanging out with a friend of mine named Daniel. We found ourselves on Ben Yehuda Street, named after the father of modern Hebrew, Eliezer Ben-Yehuda. On Shabbat in

Jerusalem, everything closed down—including public trans-port, shops, banks and markets. It was a well-earned day of rest for a weary city, ready to be rebooted. On Sundays, the first day of the Israeli workweek, the city would open again, and everyone would stream out onto the sloped cobblestone streets to congregate and celebrate. The day Daniel and I found ourselves on Ben Yehuda was one of those days. Amidst the flurry of activity, I saw a man who was severely disabled, both mentally and physically. He must have been in his 30s or 40s, and he was moving the wheelchair slowly and painstakingly using a joystick he maneuvered with his mouth.

The man was looking off into the distance at a cotton candy stand that had a line in front of it. Something in his eyes struck me. He evidently wanted some cotton candy but because he couldn't move very well, he likely concluded that getting it would be far too much work. I'm not sure what came over me, but I got in line myself, bought the cotton candy, walked over to the man with it and started feeding him. He tried to speak to me, but even speaking was too chal-lenging for him. All the same, it turned out I'd been right—he had wanted candy. When it was over, and I went back to my friend Daniel, he couldn't believe what he'd seen. I was supposed to be the wild man while he was supposed to be the devoutly religious one, yet here I was doing random acts of kindness. In all fairness, I wasn't entirely clear what was happening with me either!

It seemed that all the traveling and culture I was experi-encing was opening my eyes to the beauty and depth of a world I'd never fully seen before, even though it had been there the whole time. Out of my home environment, I could finally see life in layers of meaning. Still, whatever revelations I was having came to a screeching halt when I got a phone call from back home. It was David Zarabi.

"David, what's up, brother?" I answered, excited to tell him all my stories. All I could hear on the other end was sobbing. My stomach dropped.

"What's wrong?" I asked. He couldn't get the words out in full sentences. He told me his brother Mikey had been murdered—shot and killed in Little Neck, one town over from Great Neck. The murderer was one of Mikey's friends, someone who had first killed his own parents and buried them in the basement. All at once, whatever fanciful thoughts I was having before the call evaporated. David was more than a friend to me; he was like a brother. I felt his pain like it was my own.

"His funeral is tomorrow," he told me. As part of Jewish law, the deceased were to be buried as soon as possible, though not on Shabbat. Though I couldn't be home for the burial, I knew that David's family and friends would be sitting shiva together for seven days and that I could make every effort to support them for that. To start, I called my dad and told him I'd be coming home.

"Don't come home, Daniel," he told me. "You're in Israel, and what's done is done. There's nothing you can do for them here." I knew his sentiments stemmed from his practicality and sobering life experiences but not from heartlessness. Even so, the decision not to be by my friend's side during this devastating experience did not sit well with me.

"With all due respect, Dad, there is something I can do," I said. "I can come home and be there for David and his family." I got on a flight later that week, landed in New York

City and had Kurt drive me back to my old family home. My parents were happy to see me when I walked in, but they knew I hadn't just come home for pleasantries. An unmistakable heaviness hung in the room.

"David's family is sitting shiva," I said, "we have to go be with them." Both my parents' faces fell—maybe they hoped that even if I was coming home to support David that they wouldn't have to face his family's grief beside me. "We have to go be with them," I repeated. The room was silent. All the energy my arrival had generated was gone like it had been sucked out of the air with a vacuum.

"Daniel, I can't go over there," my father said quietly. The room seemed to constrict around us. I'd thought supporting David and his family was a more than reasonable request; now, I could see I'd asked for the one thing that was nearly impossible for my father to provide. My whole childhood, my father had been strong and silent, with an unimaginably high pain threshold compared to most people. My parents put on brave, cheerful faces and went at life with gusto, but underneath was a loss that haunted them both.

When I was three years old, my oldest sister Tammy had been killed. She had been crossing the road on her bicycle and was hit by a van. She had given me so much love during my critical first years and was an irreplaceable part of our family, but the tragedy was that I had hardly gotten a chance to know her or more so that she did not get to live out a promising and fulfilling life. My sister Alisa had been a little older when it happened and had more memories than I did, but it wasn't a topic anyone was eager to discuss. The void created by Tammy's death had shaken my family to the core, but we were trying to carry on regardless. My family's experience seeing Tammy pass meant that we all knew how precious and fragile life could be. There was no need to relive that pain if we didn't have to; by extension, grief became a room my family had no desire to enter.

My mother left the room and busied herself with other things, and my father got ready to do the same, as if the conversation were settled. Growing up, my dad didn't spend money on frivolous things or talk much about his feelings. He showed love by creating a safe and stable home for us in contrast to the war-torn Europe he'd left behind. Opening any kind of deep pain threatened to open it all, so mostly we never pried. Still, this was different.

"I know it's hard," I said, "but that's why we have to do it." Every force in my body was telling me to leave the room or drop the conversation, and I was nearly shaking trying to stay in place. The idea of going to my friend's house and breaking down crying in front of everyone made me shudder —in our society and among men, it was a social boundary I wasn't sure I could cross. Still, like I'd experienced on Ben Yehuda Street, I felt a deep inner calling that pushed me forward.

"They need people in their house who can understand what they're going through," I told my dad. "People who can be there with them. We have to go over there, and we have to go now."

My father paused and broke eye contact with me, sitting in a shadowed part of our living room. I could sense his guts grinding inside him because he knew I was right. After a long pause, he rose from his chair, got his jacket and walked into the bright, crisp air outside to drive us to David's.

It's hard to describe what it felt like walking into David's house that day. I hugged him, and we both cried violently. Everyone was crying, and the air felt as weighted as a wool blanket. Even my father could not hold back his tears. There was no room for small talk, no room for much of anything— except to be present for David and his family, so they knew they weren't alone.

I stayed by David's side as my father went to talk to David's parents. I noticed that Dad's walk and posture were different; even surrounded by all that heaviness, there was a gentleness in his steps I hadn't often seen before. As he crossed the living room, he turned to close a door, and our eyes met. It was like I was meeting the boy behind my father's eyes as clearly as I ever had, if only for a moment. Then the door quietly closed, and he was gone again, secreted away to an inner world only he could understand.

2

BACK TO THE MAINLAND

After finishing my year abroad in Jerusalem, I returned to SUNY Albany with a Judaic Studies minor and switched my major to English. Immediately, I was far more engaged than I'd ever been in business classes.

I gobbled up the Romantic poets like Wordsworth, Keats, Byron and Shelley, along with experimental writing by Irish writers like James Joyce and Samuel Beckett. On the spiritual side, Hermann Hesse's *Siddhartha* and *Steppenwolf* brought everything together for me, steeping philosophy in narrative. When I finished my undergraduate degree in 1993, I had a new goal: I would write the next Great American Novel.

I decided to move back to Great Neck, live with my parents, work whatever odd jobs I could to make money and spend the rest of the time establishing my literary career. Of course, it wasn't long before my dad was prodding me again.

"So, what's next, Daniel?" he asked.

"I'm giving myself a year to work and make some

money," I said. "But I'm going to do a lot of writing and see if I have a future in that." It didn't hurt that the attic rent was free, save for my father's proselytizing about choosing a career path.

"What happened to entrepreneurship and real estate?" he asked. "Maybe go to law school to get your foot in the door?"

I'm sure my dad still had his doubts about what direction my life would take, and it likely appeared as if I was delaying my next major life decision (which in retrospect, I was). I knew once my dad put his mind to me getting more education, I would never hear the end of it, so I tried to hold him off for as long as I could.

"I just want to get some real-life experience in the working world, Dad," I told him.

To stay busy, I got a job in a wholesale chemical sales room "dialing for dollars," but something felt off about it even from the day I drove up to Long Island to interview.

The sales floor was a dingy-looking boiler room-type setting with a few other disheveled guys sitting at flimsy desks, some young and some older worn dogs. On the other side of the room was a one-way mirror with an unscrupulous salesman behind it, watching us make calls all day. His name was Harvey, and he took me into a side room. As he explained it, the job was selling industrial chemicals to people all over the US—things like pavement cleaner and hose and gear

cleaner—and he hired me on the spot. He also gave me a call script.

His smile was phony enough to make a politician blush, but the instructions were simple, so I jumped right in. I got to pick my own sales name, and since I was still in love with the idea of being the next great novelist, I opted for Daniel Hemingway. The salesroom had a huge wall with balloons tacked onto it, each labeled with different sales hurdles—things like "first sale of the day," "largest sale" and so on. Whenever someone filled one of the requirements, they could pop the balloon for a prize coupon inside for things like a wireless phone or a stereo on top of sales commissions, which could get hefty. Whenever I had someone on the hook, it was always the same few lines:

"Sir, I am going to crack open a case of hose and gear cleaner and send you out five concentrated gallons for the price of three—and if I can lock in your purchase now, I'm going to include a keychain flashlight for you as a token of my appreciation. What is that PO number so I can get this started for you?"

From the very beginning, it was a shady gig. I didn't know it right away, but the products we were selling were outside of regulatory scope, and the people we were selling to were simpler folks. It wasn't real sales at all; it was bottom fishing. To make the experience worse, if one of us got a willing customer on the line, Harvey wouldn't always give us more sales script—sometimes he'd just snatch the phone away and finish the call himself. I tried to convince myself to calm down and stay focused. This was just what I had to do: suck it up, get a little experience and find time to channel my energy into better things.

A few months in, I noticed a door in the building that I hadn't seen before. While I was on break, I discreetly went over, checked to make sure no one was watching and peered in. Inside was another sales room of "senior" guys who were calling people the main room had just called, only now, they were manipulating them into buying all kinds of things they didn't need based on false pretenses. I could feel my face flush—I already felt crooked about what was going on in the front room, but this was another level. The whole business model was based on taking advantage of people, and I was helping. Feeling a visceral disdain for their inauthentic business practices, I quit that day.

Working that job the whole summer had been demoralizing, but every night, I tried to keep my mind on writing. Whenever I got home, I would read, journal and try out poetry and prose. After quitting the job, I looked through everything I'd written to see what I had, but the results of my efforts were only reams of notes and scribblings (and a few good poems, actually). The next Great American Novel hadn't materialized, and before long, my dad was on me again.

"You've got to think about your future," he said to me. "Look at your sister—she went to law school, and now she's a lawyer."

"I don't want to go to law school, Dad," I told him. "What do I need it for? If I want to be an author, I'll write books. If I want to be an entrepreneur or go into real estate, I'll do that instead."

"Look," he said bluntly, "right now, you have no plan. You don't have money to buy real estate. You don't have any experience. Your sister Alisa is a lawyer, and so many doors are opening for her. She's building important relationships."

"I can make relationships on my own," I replied—though in the back of my mind, I knew I couldn't really count pot-smoking telemarketers from Long Island as desirable relationships.

"What I'm saying is, why wouldn't you go get a degree?" he asked, ignoring me. "While you're at it, you can explore the city, look at potential investment properties and see what it might mean to convert your aspirations into something real. Just get the degree first—and get a master's in business to supplement it."

We had countless persuasive (and often one-sided) conversations about higher education in our kitchen throughout the summer, but I had to admit, he was pointing out things I hadn't seen before. If I went to law school, I could meet ambitious people, network and get into some exciting idea exchanges. I could start thinking about entrepreneurship while building a career for myself—and if I needed to, I could get an MBA to take me to the next level. His ultimate message was simple: get a law degree, then pivot. It was what my sister did, and it would work for me as well.

I was still resistant; I thought I was *done* with school. My education had been stifling enough up to that point, but what could be more stifling than law school? Even so, writing clearly wasn't working out, and what Dad was saying made sense. As ever, he persuaded me to see his way.

With my sister Alisa's help framing out and line-editing my application essays, I sent in my application to New York Law School in Tribeca and hoped for the best. She had always been a staunch supporter of mine—and she knew that because of my restless nature, I could always use some additional encouragement. After waiting for a month or two, I got a letter back that I'd been accepted.

It meant that even though I wouldn't be far away, I would no longer be living at home either. To send me off in style, we all sat down together for a nice dinner. After plenty of back and forth, it seemed to my family that I was finally set on a defined path forward.

"Just remember, Daniel," my dad said. "Always choose your friends wisely. Choosing the wrong friends can get you into trouble quickly, and it is much easier to get into trouble than it is to get out of it."

———

After my parents saw me off, I moved into an off-campus apartment in Battery Park City with another graduate student named Evan Freifeld as my roommate in 1994. Evan was a sincere guy who was a few years older than me. He was much more serious about his studies than I was; for my part, I was more intent on experiencing city life to the fullest and trading stocks often as I could. I had always had a private love affair with Manhattan from a distance, but being in the middle of it was the most energizing thing imaginable.

Though I was prepared for dense reading, I wasn't prepared for the weight of the tomes I'd have to carry— lugging my backpack around law school felt like I was in Egypt dragging bricks to the pyramids. Still, my Judaic Studies background came in particularly useful since reading legal analysis was not all that different from reading scholarly analysis of the Torah and the Talmud, as it turned out.

I rapidly adjusted to absorbing huge volumes of legal cases, but the environment was a turnoff. For the most part, it was hyper-competitive, petty and careerist. What I was learning didn't feel all that useful; it was all theory and no practical skills. It felt like I was being given keys without knowing which locks they went into. If I was going to be a lawyer, I wanted to understand how civil procedure worked in real life, not in a vacuum.

In my second year, I applied to work for New York State Supreme Court Judge Edward H. Lehner. He was a tall, bald man known for his firm yet mild-mannered demeanor, and I knew him as one of the wiser figures on the New York State Supreme Court. He was also known for his real estate acumen and for combining his law judgments with facts and real-world experience. He was recognized and respected, and I was eager to learn from him.

Everything happened in the downtown New York State Supreme Courthouse at 60 Centre Street, next to the criminal court, the federal courthouse and "the tombs," where they temporarily housed criminals. In New York, there are always hundreds of active real estate cases at any given time, and Judge Lehner's courtroom worked on many of them. All of them were at least somewhat interesting (to me, at any rate), but one of my case assignments towered above the rest: Donald Trump vs. Leona Helmsley, through their respective business entities.

In 1995, Donald Trump and Leona Helmsley were absolute titans of New York City real estate. Helmsley was a real estate billionaire, hotelier and figurehead at the Helmsley Organization. She was married to Harry Helmsley, a giant in his own right—the guy was basically the Mickey Mantle of early real estate syndication and development in New York City. As former POTUS, Donald Trump needs no introduction, but it's worth saying that in the 1990s, he was a business icon of nearly mythic proportions who amassed a fortune from a smaller one and got a lot of cool shit done in New York City.

It was a case where Trump was suing the Helmsley Organization and indirectly the "Queen of Mean," Leona Helmsley, to terminate a ground lease she held over the Empire State Building. The backstory was that the building had been sold to Japanese billionaire real estate investor Hideki Yokoi in the late 1980s, who then gave it to his daughter Kiiko Nakahara. Though Nakahara and her husband owned the building, Leona Helmsley had a ground lease on it that limited what they could do with their asset. To create more value, they reasoned they could have Leona Helmsley's lease broken to establish more control over the entire asset, but they needed an experienced New York real estate mogul to help them accomplish that. To do so, Nakahara and her husband turned to Trump and gave him a 50 percent interest in the building in exchange for working his magic and getting Leona Helmsley out to unlock so much dormant value.

Throughout the case, I sat behind the bench with the clerks and police watching Trump and Helmsley (in her case, sometimes her proxies) file in and out of the courtroom, always accompanied by their respective panels of big-shot lawyers (plus a bodyguard, in Trump's case). As the case developed, Trump argued that the Helmsleys were in violation of their lease because they had turned a once-iconic New York landmark into little more than a vertical slum (with particular attention paid to the mice that constantly roamed the building's dark hallways). Though there were clear financial motivations involved in the case, beneath the surface was a bitter rivalry between the Helmsley and Trump families, two of the city's great real estate dynasties. I had never been particularly passionate about the practice of law, but I had always coveted real estate—and in this case, I saw a perfect escape route.

"Judge Lehner," I said one day, "as you know, I love real estate and hope to be an investor one day. I've been studying the legal side of property, but now I want to learn the business side. With your permission, I'd love to approach Mr. Trump at some point in the courtroom." It was after a long day, and Judge Lehner was stepping out of his formal robes into street clothes. I had always known him to be a sharp and gentle man whose opinions I respected immensely, but now I was anxious to hear what he would say. He considered a moment before he answered me. "I've got no problem with that," he replied, "but if you're going to approach him, you can't sit behind the bench with me during their proceedings. You'll have to sit in the gallery like everyone else." That worked for me.

The next time Trump came in, I sat in the audience and tapped my foot until the day's proceedings were over. When Judge Lehner struck his gavel to adjourn, I was out of my seat and trailing Trump and his entourage towards the elevators. One of his burly security guys spotted me right away, partially screening me from my target. They were standing at the building elevators when I caught up to them. His guard towered over me (which was not too difficult with me standing 5'8") as I steeled myself for a literal elevator pitch.

"Mr. Trump, my name is Daniel Lebensohn," I said, jockeying for some clear air around the guard. "I'm a graduate student at New York Law School, sir, and I'd love to work for your organization. I'm passionate about real estate and think I could add real value." Before I could finish my pitch, Trump was already in the elevator, and I was being brushed off, but I wasn't about to give up.

As the doors closed, I raced down the stairs to beat Trump and his entourage to the bottom floor where a chauffeur-driven limo was waiting. I made it out to the limo before they did, and as they approached, I set into my sales pitch all over again. This time, I got his attention.

"Look, kid," he said to me, hardly concealing his irritation, "why don't you send your resumé over to my office?" I was still being shooed off, but it wasn't a no.

"Not only will I do that, sir," I said to him, "but I'll be sure to indicate in my cover letter that you suggested I do so!"

Donald Trump couldn't have cared less what I indicated in my cover letter, but he waved at me all the same, got in his limo and was off. I couldn't stop smiling—I had just met Donald Trump! Truthfully, I was more impressed by my own effort than I was focused on the outcome of our exchange. I hadn't even finished law school, but I was already getting exposure to some titans of New York real estate! I was beyond stoked.

I sent my resumé over with a carefully crafted letter. The possibility of getting such a huge opportunity kept me excited, and I was glad I'd engaged so directly, but I heard nothing back. After that, I sent another letter and made some phone calls to follow up—still nothing. Finally, I figured I would go up to Trump headquarters in person—I had nothing to lose, after all. I subwayed and walked to Trump

Tower on 5th Avenue, a heavily guarded building if ever there was one. I was marching into the lobby with my chest out and on my way to the elevators when I was intercepted.

"Where are you going?" the guard said sternly, trying to grab my arm.

"I'm here to see Mr. Trump," I said as confidently as I could. The guard laughed. "Sure you are," he said. With that, he spun me around and marched me back out into the street.

After that failed attempt, I called a few more times and left messages with HR. A few weeks later, I received my official rejection letter:

Thanks for the inquiry, but we're not hiring at this time.

I knew it was a moonshot and was a little disappointed, but I still appreciated the definitive "no." I was glad I'd seen it through all the way to the end; unfortunately, it seemed that I would have to do the same with law school.

———

When I wasn't working or studying, I was taking my dad's advice: riding around Washington Heights on my mountain bike, looking at buildings and learning as many brokers' names as I could. I knew there were legacies and nuances behind every piece of property I saw. Though there was a long list of required classes for a law degree, I took business electives whenever I could or traded stocks in the Stuyvesant Hall study lounge to whet my appetite. I was fantasizing about what I'd do with my own huge apartment building once I became a player in the real estate world.

In 1996, Evan told me he was getting engaged and that I

would be losing his half of the rent on our apartment. At the time, I had been bar-backing at a dive on the lower west side of Chelsea called Red Rock West three nights a week. It was a biker and cop joint that boasted gorgeous bartenders, cheap drinks and lots of fist fights. My duties included bringing cases up from the basement, cleaning glasses and doing all kinds of other prep work—but on good nights I was leaving with $200 to $500 in cash tips. It was like getting paid to party, pick up girls and drink for free—but even though the money coming in was good, I didn't want to pay for rent in Manhattan by myself. Fortunately, I got a call from Ari around the same time that he was thinking of moving to the city.

"I want to get back in the action," Ari said. "I've been in Atlantic Beach for a while, but I could expand my business down there and would be closer to my office. If you're open to it, we should move in together! It would be a fantastic way to share costs, and we'd have a blast."

I was immediately on board—it was a chance to move in with my best friend who I'd known since age three (and who had since become a rather legendary bachelor in the area). After a short phone call, we agreed to start looking at places. My dad's tenant, Steve Harris, was the one to show us around. Steve had shifty blue eyes, bushy white hair and a demeanor that was reminiscent of Rodney Dangerfield. Even though Steve was renting a modest home from my dad, it wasn't because he lacked financial resources—he was a former lawyer turned investor who trusted nobody and was constantly panting like a dog in heat after years of chain-smoking. He only rented because he wanted to save on expenses and pour his money into New York real estate, which he made all too clear to us during the apartment tours.

"Boys, I keep all my money in bricks," he said in his hoarse voice. "That way, my wife can't spend it." Steve had his own mini-empire in the form of seven or eight walkup apartment buildings in the East Village, but a few of the places he showed us were subterranean pits nobody would want to live in. All the same, he had his own opinions about them.

"This place is perfect for you two!" he said a little too urgently. "Listen, Danny, if you don't take this place? Fuck you. You're an asshole. And Ari? Fuck you too."

After a few more misses, Steve showed us another apartment on East 88th Street on the northwest corner of 88th Street and 1st Avenue. It was an old tenement building with Luigi's Pizzeria on the ground floor, a place that had been around New York since the 1980s. The building had a wide stairwell, and the apartment was all the way on the fourth floor. It was quite a walk, and Steve's Marlboro-addled lungs were having a hard time with it.

"You guys go on up and look at it," he panted, putting the keys in my hand. "I'll be right up."

The apartment had a long, skinny hallway running into a skinny kitchen with a window into 1st Avenue. There was a modest bathroom and a snug bedroom. Down the hall was a sizable living room with a fire escape and additional windows. The place was $880 a month, and it was the best one Steve had shown us. Ari and I were both excited—it wasn't anything too fancy, but the price and the location were unbeatable!

On the way out of the building, we told Steve we were

interested as he was getting into his white Cadillac. He nodded excitedly before catching himself.

"Great, great—but listen," he said conspiratorially. "I showed you this, so you're not going to cut me out right? My wife and I are leasing agents here, and we get a commission, so you're not going to fuck me, right?"

"Steve, relax," I said. "Nobody's fucking anybody." How Ari and I would even know how to screw Steve out of his commission was beyond me—let alone that even if we had wanted to, he was still my father's tenant! Steve's paranoia aside, Ari and I signed our lease and moved in together.

3

LIFE IN THE TIME OF DOT-COM OPTIMISM

Because Ari already had a reasonably successful business and I was still getting established, we agreed that he would pay slightly more in rent than I would; in exchange, he would get the bedroom while I made part of the communal space my own. To make it work, I brought a bed in and sectioned off part of the living area. It didn't allow for much privacy, but Ari and I promised to be conscientious of one another.

Ari and I usually weren't home at the same times, as he was usually jetting around the city with an attaché case full of artwork under his arm. Ari bought and sold art prints to collectors all around the city, and he often brought his paintings and illustrations home for us both to admire. He had offices set up in Fairview, New Jersey, but sourced a lot of his business from California. In the early years of animation before digitization, major animation studios like Disney made all their animations with hand-drawn frames called "cels." Once the cels were drawn and filmed, all the drawings were thrown in the dumpsters—but many animators took them out of the trash to keep as souvenirs or to resell later. Ari was hunting those animators down via word of mouth and buying their illustrations with the intention of reselling them for profit.

The significant amount of money he was making at the time made me reasonably envious, but I mostly admired his work ethic and vision. I also couldn't get enough of the art he brought home and was impressed by his encyclopedic knowledge of it. Whenever I took notice of one of his cels, he would instantly recount its provenance.

"Ah, yes," he said fondly, "that's from the fifth season of *The Flintstones* in 1964 when Betty was yelling at Barney for not feeding their dinosaur, Hoppy."

Even if he knew everything about animation, he was up to date on contemporary art as well. Whenever we weren't at work or throwing parties in our apartment, we went to the Art Expo near the West Side Highway. If he didn't have a booth there himself, he was going to other booths to make deals. It was opening my eyes to how much art and creativity there was in the city, and I was fascinated that there was such a market for it. On one occasion at an outdoor market in Chelsea, I even bought a signed Alexander Calder print for $125. It was a lot of money at the time, but I thought of it as an investment.

When I finally graduated from New York Law School in 1997, I finished with a C+ average—which was definitely not enough to get me into a white shoe law firm. Even so, I hadn't gotten rejected by Donald Trump or sat through three years of migraine-inducing legalese just to give up. I had the idea that I might be able to backdoor my way into a better law firm that was above my academic station if I applied through a temp agency. I did so, and sure enough, I secured a job as a paralegal at Graham & James.

Graham & James was a firm located in the now-infamous Lipstick Building in Midtown Manhattan, where Bernie Madoff had two or three floors to himself. The work they did was mostly on mortgage-backed securities, and it gave me exposure to the kinds of high-caliber deals I was hungry for.

On the first day, they gave me a shitty cubicle and told me to start digging into titles and surveys. Because I was getting paid hourly, I was moved between many different commercial real estate projects in the practice and got a chance to work with every associate and many partners, absorbing details about the firm in a broader way than any one associate ever could. Each one of the partners was assigned to one primary vertical within commercial real estate and several projects within that space, and they were always treading water just to keep up. At the time, I was a temp—I didn't have the pressure, but I had all the flexibility and got the truest sense of an education while getting to bill each of my work hours. Before long, I was managing the diligence on multi-state deals and learning everything I could.

I'd been hired as a paralegal with the promise that if I worked hard, I'd make an associate—but that quickly seemed like it wasn't going to happen. I was buried in files and being worked to the bone by the senior partners, which was all part of the company culture. Fortunately, Richard Liebman was a little different.

"Daniel, what are you doing for lunch today?" he asked me one day—I must've seemed particularly harried.

"No plans today, Richard," I replied. "Probably going to work through." Richard waved his hand in the air.

"Forget that! Put your files down. I'm taking you to lunch." In an office where the senior partners were usually so busy with their own affairs, Richard's kindness was refreshing and much appreciated. Over sushi that day, Richard talked about every topic imaginable at our firm— what projects were giving him a headache, what the partners were saying and so on. I shared that I'd been hopeful of moving up in the firm but that I didn't seem to be making much progress.

"Don't worry about that yet, Danny," he said calmly. "I know this is an overwhelming environment for a lot of people, so just focus on the hard work. Learn your stuff and get to know everybody as much as you can. And don't worry about the partners—your time will come." The friction I was experiencing at the firm was that the promise of making partner or advancing in the firm was always being dangled like a carrot, but it was unclear who would make it (or if you were actually wanted at the top). After lunch with Richard that day and on other days to come, I began to see him as a friend and a mentor. I was relieved that there was somebody who *did* want me to advance and who I could confide in. I resolved to take his advice: focus on the work and build relationships.

A lot of the files that came through at Graham & James were classic New York closings, situations where one guy was selling, one guy was buying and everyone was in the same room together—both teams' attorneys, paralegals, financiers, title guys, lenders, lenders' attorneys and brokers. The scope of these deals was enormous, and the energy in the room was always frenetic; deals could take a day, a week or multiple weeks, depending on the size of the transaction. In the case of the Helmsley Building on 230 Park Avenue, the negotiations stretched on and on.

The deal was that Richard Kalikow, a prominent real estate player in New York City, was buying the building with his young partner Adam Hochfelder, and we were representing the lender financing for Kalikow's team. It was a $225 million deal, and there were about 20 people in the room. A classic New York City-style closing was underway, with a room full of lawyers and financial wizards riffing together—it was like a jazz improv session played in the key of commercial real estate. After a bout of fierce debate about how assets would be delivered and uncollected rents would be adjusted between parties, lawyers would rush into a side room to crunch numbers and then re-enter with new figures. The title guys were marking and managing title clearance issues, and sponsors were ticking and tying all ends to push it through to a close. These deals were never a small feat, and there were always complications. They required many hands on deck and a captain's navigation skills.

It was intense and exciting, but as much as I loved being in those rooms, I hated the grind—and I could see the long and punishing road ahead of me. I was making money, but I was working from 7 am to 11 pm every day. Even if the associates and partners were getting paid more than I was, they were working the exact same hours (and sometimes even more). Even though they'd clawed their way to the top, they were still here hunched over their desks and away from their families after everyone else had gone home. Many of the partners were constantly red in the face and on their second (or third) marriages—some even needed open heart surgery in their 50s. These people had money, power and prestige, but they didn't have what I viewed as success. They were trapped, and I intended to avoid their fate as much as possible.

While some of my friends were going out to dinner and celebrating the end of law school, I stayed at home and studied my ass off for the bar exam. I may have been busting my ass at the bottom of the totem pole, networking and learning all the nuances of real estate deals, but after all that work, I intended for it to pay off—*huge*. In those conference rooms, sandwiched between countless high-powered people sweating and screaming at each other over real estate nuances, I experienced the greatest moment of clarity I had had up to that point of my life. I did not want to be one of a hundred people huddled around the negotiating table; I wanted to be the guy sitting at the head of it—the one taking the risks, putting the team together and leaving the room with the trophy.

After months of Graham & James drudgery and angling to escape the rat race, I was awaiting the results of my bar exam. I was a working paralegal, but I wasn't officially a lawyer until the results came back. At home, I still had my notes papered up everywhere—in my bedroom, the bathroom, above my kitchen table—from when I was studying to remind me of my goal. On each one, I'd scrawled a simple message: *NEVER AGAIN*.

I was at work when the results were finally posted online. As I scanned the list of new attorneys, my heart sank: my name was nowhere to be found. *Oh shit*, I thought. *This can't be happening*. The prospect of being stuck at Graham

& James forever *and* studying for the bar exam again was unfolding before me, though fortunately, my nightmare didn't come true—there was another practical exam whose results hadn't been posted yet, and as a result, my name was just printed on another list.

"I passed!" I shouted at my secretary, scooping her up and giving her an impulsive hug and a kiss. Now that I was officially a lawyer in good standing with the New York State Bar Association, Graham & James expanded my role and started paying me more. The timing was good because Ari's business was doing so well that he was ready to get a bigger place for himself, and I now had enough money coming in to float our apartment by myself. Sure enough, he signed the lease over to me, and I helped him move to an apartment on 86th and 2nd Avenue a few blocks away.

Shortly after Ari moved out in late 1997, I met a girl named Jackie. We'd been set up by my old friend Eric Newman and his fiancée Randy, and we went out to a local bar to have a few drinks. Jackie was five years older than me, but she was energetic, fun and always positive. I liked her right away—she was a real guy's girl, and the entire time we talked about business and entrepreneurship. I was surprised by how many points of connectivity we had, and after a few good dates, we officially became a couple.

Internet businesses in New York City were exploding at the time, and Jackie was a part of that wave. She was working at About.com and knew a deep network of tech people, internet entrepreneurs and other white-collar professionals who were established around the city—and as we went to parties and local bars together, I was meeting more and more of them.

I later got word that the apartment next door was opening up. At the same time, Kurt had just called off an ephemeral engagement—but he was still living with his ex-fiancée and hadn't found new living arrangements. Now, he was looking for a new place in New York to make a fresh start as quickly as he could.

"You have to move in next door!" I told him over the phone. "The building is great, and it's an amazing location. We can be roommates without being roommates!"

"Sounds great," Kurt said in response. "Good thing there's a wall between us, or we'd be at each other's throats in a month."

As soon as Kurt moved in, it was like being back in high school again, except this time, the city was our playground. We had few cares other than studying and making enough money to cover rent, bar tabs and the parties we threw from time to time. Just like we used to, Kurt and I fell into a routine of working out every day. After our exercise, we would get Wiener schnitzel at Mocca, a Hungarian restaurant on 2nd Avenue near where we lived. Some days, I would even overindulge and talk Kurt into getting a second order to share, which always made him laugh.

Another favorite spot of ours was Sammy's Roumanian Steakhouse, a Lower East Side restaurant that served Jewish and Eastern European food. It had a big, faded metal sign out front that was painted yellow and red, and the downstairs area was only partly manufactured. The tiled ceilings were seven-and-a-half feet tall, and between each of the tiles were crammed hundreds of business cards from local vendors and patrons that always fell onto the floor. The food was heavy and delicious but eating there

meant accepting a resting layer of liquified fat on the tables
—not to mention the musical stylings of Dani Luv, the
house musician from Israel who played synthesizer in the
basement for 22 years. With a lurching rendition of "Hava
Nagila" playing in the background, Kurt, David and I
discussed our business plans, ambitions and the general
hysterics of our lives over kishka, foot-long hanger steaks,
stuffed cabbage and bottles of vodka encased in blocks
of ice.

"Things at Graham & James are going well, but I'm
ready for something else," I told Kurt between bites. He
nodded vigorously.

"I'm feeling the same way," he replied. "Why don't you
put your feelers out? You've got the experience. There's got
to be a better shop for you out there."

"I don't even want to practice law if I'm being honest," I
replied. "I want a business of my own." Kurt nodded.

"I'm not sure I want to be a banker my whole life,
either," he said. Behind us, Dani Luv switched on a rotating
disco ball that swept pale rainbow-colored lights across our
faces and started clapping out a rhythm (in which a few
older patrons weakly joined).

Our appetite was understandable. Kurt and I were cut
from the same cloth and were similarly grinding it out to
establish ourselves in the city; Ari, on the other hand, had
already established himself and his business seemed to be
thriving. In short, we were taking the subway while he was
driving models around Chelsea in his Porsche. It was more
than enough to motivate us both to pursue our own ends.

As a newly minted lawyer practicing in the state of New
York, I was getting antsy. Kurt was right—even though I

appreciated the money I was making at Graham & James, I wanted to grow.

After our lunch that day, I discreetly shopped myself around and landed an interview with Nomura Holdings, a Japanese company that trades globally in financial securities. For my part, I was particularly interested in their real-estate dealings. At the time, a guy named Ethan Penner was working at Nomura's bond desk and running their commercial real estate endeavors. Penner was one of the later-generation bond kings—later in comparison to people like Michael Milken, who rose to financial stardom for his leveraging of high-yield bonds (commercial bonds issued by companies with lower credit ratings or unestablished credit histories) in the 1980s. Penner was an innovative guy who helped pioneer the market for commercial mortgage-backed securities—and later on, he was even involved in securitizing Bon Jovi's musical rights. He could spin money out of seemingly anything, and the opportunity to learn from him was tantalizing.

The interview went well, and they made me a six-figure offer. Though I already had a job, they were a huge financial firm offering more money and a way out of law—how could I say no? I gave my notice at Graham & James and was excited to start the next chapter of my life—that is, until I got another letter in the mail:

Mr. Daniel Lebensohn, thank you again for your interest in a position at Nomura Holdings. Unfortunately, as a result of internal restructuring, the position has been eliminated, and our offer is thus rescinded.

I couldn't believe what I was reading and thought there must have been some mistake—I'd already given notice at my job and was set to start in weeks! In a matter of minutes, I'd gone from having a promising future at a major firm involved in commercial real estate transactions to potentially being unemployed. *If you couldn't count on an offer from a major firm like Nomura,* I thought to myself, *what could you count on?* I spoke to Jackie about what had happened and how disappointed I was.

"I would meet you for lunch, but I'm busy today," she said. "Why don't you get lunch with Paul? He deals with this kind of thing all the time and might be able to help. We can get dinner later, and you can get me up to speed."

Jackie was right—our mutual friend Paul was an experienced corporate lawyer who specialized in contract law, and there was clearly something amiss about how things had gone down. I called him to meet me at a local sushi bar and printed out the communication I'd had with Nomura. After weighing it over, he had a suggestion.

"I think you have a case here," he said. "They terminated their written offer with you. I think you can recover money damages." As Paul clearly explained, it was an open-and-shut case of breach of contract. If we were to come to a settlement, whatever the figure was would mean nothing to Nomura, but it would mean the world to me.

"If you really think this is a good idea," I said, "would you mind writing something to Nomura's HR department as my lawyer?" He agreed and drafted a series of letters detailing how the firm had broken their commitment, noting that I'd be pursuing damages if the situation wasn't swiftly resolved. It didn't take long for Nomura to get in touch with me directly.

"Daniel!" a bright voice on the other end of the phone

said. "Listen, we've reviewed your file, and we regret the way things ended. If you're available, we'd love to have you come in and discuss some options so we all can avoid litigation. I'm sure we can work this out to everyone's mutual satisfaction."

After a few meetings, they tendered my attorney and me a gesture payment in lieu of a drawn-out court battle. In the end, I walked away with $18,000—I couldn't have thanked Paul enough! Though I would miss the opportunity to learn from Ethan Penner's cunning business mind, the situation underscored something I'd sensed about the world from early on: I couldn't depend on the good reputation of a company or on any gatekeeper for my own financial security. Fortunately, the settlement I'd received was significant enough to make a serious run at entrepreneurship so I could support myself independently. I took it as another sign from the universe: I wasn't meant to thrive in a corporate environment, and I would have to make my own way.

4

THE HAZARDS OF BEING AHEAD OF THE CURVE

After paying off some delinquent bills, I set into developing a killer business idea. Whatever it was, I wanted it to ride the swell of enthusiasm I saw happening in New York's tech sector.

Though I was not an early zealot of the web or overly tech-literate, I knew the internet was a world-changing development that was huge and exciting. It was a super-highway that was going to bring all kinds of different industries into the future. Numerous dot-com businesses started popping up in the city with sky-high valuations, but for the most part, commercial real estate seemed like it was being left behind. As I brainstormed, I kept returning to how antiquated the real estate industry was and how powerful it would be to put together a technologically advanced brokerage, a kind of online marketplace for real estate buyers and sellers.

New York City was the real estate capital of the world, and yet the way deals were done there was so inefficient and old-fashioned. Brokerages would send out a mass email with a set-up on a piece of property, and it would get sent to the company's entire email list—but the people who received the email often didn't even qualify for it. What the real estate world needed was a system that used technology to put listings in front of potential buyers, but more specifically, to *qualified* buyers. It would be like eBay for real estate: it wouldn't house anything, and it wouldn't have any inventory. It would simply connect buyers and sellers through the internet, and it would be called BuildingBrokers.com.

I reached out to some tech people and programmers in Jackie's network about what it would take to build something like that, taking notes on what they had to say. Before long, it was clear that executing my concept was possible with the money I had—and that there was a definite gap in the market for the product I envisioned. After that, I arranged another lunch with Kurt and Ari to let them know what I had in mind. Once they heard my pitch, they both had smiles on their faces.

"I think it's great, Daniel," Ari said. "New York City is the perfect place for something like this. You're ahead of the curve here."

"I agree," Kurt said. "There's so much money flowing into Silicon Alley. The market is only going up." I grinned.

"You're up next, Kurt," I said. "No more waiting tables or shoeshines soon, right?" He laughed and punched me in the shoulder harder than a good joke like that deserved. Like me, Kurt also had designs on getting his own startup off the ground called QVT, a company that involved software interactions with ATMs. Both of our ventures were in their infancy, but both had promise. Kurt raised a glass of beer, and Ari and I followed suit.

"To making our millions, right?" We echoed him and clinked glasses.

———

Though the idea was sound, there were still weeks and weeks of work to prepare, a business plan to refine, advisory board members to get together and a host of other details to frame out. I worked tirelessly and kept iterating, checking my work with other lawyers, business executives and trusted friends. At last, I started reaching out to brokers I had dealt with through my prior work in law and asking them if they wanted to get involved. Back then, stepping on brokers' toes was a major faux pas—if you circumvented them, you would get put out of business.

The first person I had to reach out to was Mike Besen of Besen & Associates, along with his entire team. Mike was an old-school investment sales broker in New York, and if anyone was going to give me a sense of brokers' appetites for a shift in their industry, it would be him. Because my proposal had the potential to disrupt the broker business, I had to offer something that was worth their time and interest, and that proved my idea was viable. Though Mike was clearly intrigued, he was still ambivalent about what benefit it would offer his business.

"I'll tell you what," I said. "Give me your hardest listings. I'll put them on my platform and get them in front of good, qualified buyers. In return, all you have to do is give me an endorsement." After talking it through, he agreed. Since my pitch had worked on Mike, I used the same strategy to pitch countless other brokers, friends and friends' fathers who owned property (one of whom was Martin Goldman, Ari's father, who owned a 2,100-acre plot of pine land in New Jersey not far from Atlantic City that he was having a particularly hard time selling).

I took pitch meetings all around the city, many of which didn't go anywhere. Sometimes the people I spoke to weren't interested right away; other times I would give my pitch, set up a second meeting to pitch them again and still get a noncommittal answer. Even though tech businesses were booming, convincing brokers and other real estate professionals to trust me and my unproven concept was one of the hardest challenges I had ever taken on. I was getting an entirely new appreciation for just how much work went into growing a business on your own.

After months and months of meetings, I had a few dozen listings that were hard to sell for one reason or another— zoning complications, heavy building restrictions, unusual locations and so on. I had a rather esoteric collection of assets, but I reasoned that it was all part of my product's pitch. With the internet's ability to unlock the right buyers and sellers, I would move even the toughest listings through my brokerage and be in the black soon enough.

Even with the Nomura settlement, I didn't have a lot of money. What I did have was an idea, some context, a deep bench of young lawyers and financiers who knew and liked me around New York City and a law degree. Just as my dad had promised, all that lawyering and relationship building had been enough to open quite a few doors. After networking at business events, prematurely hiring a tech company and building a small team, my business was up and running—and I was rapidly accruing credit card debt. In late 1998, BuildingBrokers.com was officially live.

Building Brokers was meant to be a marketplace for pre-qualified buyers that offered compelling properties with accurate, real-time data and documentation—including line items like state of the title, environmental conditions of the property, income and expenses and so on—all in one war room. I was working out of my apartment on 88th and 1st with a couple of computers and some makeshift Gantt charts papered over my desk. Beyond a successful launch of Building Brokers, I was already thinking long-term about bigger projects the company could take on down the line. Since we were positioned at the intersection of finance and technology, I instinctively knew there were a lot of ways to innovate in the space.

One plugin I began to map out was a way for users to have a fractional, tradable interest in real estate. As everyone in the business knows, a building is not a particularly liquid asset. To sell it, you have to find a broker, pay for marketing, find a buyer and so on. It takes a significant amount of time to get to the money. If there were a way that investors could own fractional pieces of real estate, I reasoned, those illiquid assets would suddenly become much more liquid, and more investors could get involved—and using the internet and data science to keep track of all that information would make it a lot more manageable. My head was bursting with ideas, and I was zipping around the city, telling them to anybody who would listen.

I hired a New York development company in the Flat-iron District to engineer all the specs and the code of the product—from how users would bid to how they would post. To get the website up and running, I hired a nearby web development company called WebSytz—seriously—who were another small shop like us and who needed the business as badly as we did.

As a severely bootstrapped operation, it was becoming clear that it might be useful to have a smart person with white hair on the team for some of the financing meetings. Having someone who was older on the team gave everyone else in the room the appearance of more experience, which in turn might make investors a little looser with their pocketbooks (that was the working theory, anyway). To do that, I reached out to my old mentor, Richard Leibman, to see if he was interested. To him, it was refreshing to apply his expertise in a different way and to still find a way to stray from the conventional path—even in his 50s. After a few short conversations, he was onboard.

"It's a good thing you're not at Graham & James anymore, Daniel," he said with a chortle, "but I didn't think I'd be working with you so soon."

With the added legitimacy of Richard on our board of directors and as a team member, we went hunting together for institutional money to keep the engine rolling down the tracks. Since I'd just used Graham & James to fill one of our board seats, I figured playing up more of my connections there could be useful. The next item on the list was to call Jeff Mitzner.

When I worked at Graham & James, Jeff was one of several outside title guys from First American Title who was often involved in many of the firm's big real estate deals. First American Title was owned by First American Financial, a public title company that I knew had an appetite for tech investments to expand their core business. Because there were no centralized online databases of information to look up property owners or other identifiers at the time, Jeff was usually the first person I called whenever I needed some hard-to-reach ownership information. As I was looking for funding in Building Brokers' first seed round, my angle now was that Jeff could connect me to financiers who could fund my project; in turn, a successful investment would bring money into the firm and make Jeff look good to all the higher-ups. It was a win-win.

"Jeff!" I said warmly over the phone, "How's the grind over there?"

"Same as ever, Daniel," he replied. "What can I do for you?"

"I heard through the grapevine that First American wants to invest in tech projects, and I had an opportunity I wanted to bring to your attention," I said. "I'm working on something cutting-edge right now that I think your colleagues will be interested in, but I wanted to go through you first. Think you could connect us?"

I set up a meeting with Jeff to expand on the opportunity in person, after which I met Jeff, the head of First American's NY branch and his business peers at their office. Although they were an older company, they had resources and were looking to innovate. They were used to closing conventional title insurance deals, but they were hungry to expand. As I expected, that included dipping their toes into the world of tech and entrepreneurship. I explained the entire business concept to their team and after a series of interviews (and on the strength of my relationship with Jeff), Building Brokers struck a deal: First American was willing to invest $600,000 in my venture for 10 percent of the company, which gave us a pre-money valuation of approximately $6,000,000.

I got the official fax of First American's signatures on Building Brokers' corporate documents while I was staying at David Zarabi's parents' house. As I showed him the sheet, he beamed at me—he was so happy that it felt like his victory too, and in a way, it was. It was such a massive win that I could hardly wrap my mind around it. My vision of fusing tech and real estate and transforming the entire market with one company was already materializing, and I was only getting started.

Although finally getting the money to fund Building Brokers in earnest felt triumphant, it came at the end of years of scrambling and countless meetings. Jackie and I had supported one another through it all, but the stress had taken its toll, and the relationship had overcooked. After four years together, we went our separate ways. Though we were saddened to see it end, we did our best to remain amicable with one another. I had cherished our time together, but I felt a little relief at being on my own again. With so many new responsibilities on my plate, things were moving very quickly, and I needed to be focused on what was ahead.

As soon as the check cleared, I started spending it to grow the business. Finally, I brought Eric Weiner onboard, an amazing sales guy who owned his own property and casualty insurance company. I had previously met Eric through Jackie, with the intention of having Eric sell our wares while merging part of his business into our online platform. I gave him equity in exchange for sweat investment capital, and before long, I was ready to spring for some office space.

Around Q2 of 1998, Building Brokers moved into the Lincoln Building at 60 East 42nd Street, a massive skyscraper directly across from Grand Central Terminal. It was surreal—in short order, I'd gotten a public company to invest in my idea, achieved a multimillion-dollar valuation, recruited a handful of experienced professionals who were materially my seniors to join me and even secured a legitimate office in a classic building in Manhattan. I had a team of approximately six people working with me, and we were ready to corner the tech side of the commercial real estate market.

For my 30th birthday that year in 2000 (and considering our mutual success), Kurt and I decided to throw the biggest costume party New York had ever seen. We hired a professional DJ to spin in my bedroom and a bartender for Kurt's apartment and told everyone on our floor to open their doors so people could stream in and out of the hallway. When I went to pick up an outfit at the costume store, I turned and saw a beautiful woman standing next to me. We made eye contact for a moment, and she smiled—and since I was in higher spirits than ever, I couldn't help myself.

"It's my birthday tonight, you know," I told her. She raised her eyebrows.

"Is that so?"

"My friend and I are turning the entire floor of our apartment into a nightclub. We've got a DJ and a bartender and everything. Whatever you're picking out, I want to see you wearing it at our place later tonight." After some back and forth, we exchanged names and numbers, and she promised she would attend. On my way out, I landed on a Roman centurion's outfit along with a cheap shield and sword. I planned to go to the party as Russell Crowe's Maximus from *Gladiator*; in light of the meteoric year I'd had, it seemed like the only appropriate option.

The DJ and bartender arrived that evening, and before long, our entire floor was a mass of sweaty moving bodies. The music was blasting, and drinks were flowing, which meant dialogue wasn't all that easy. Whenever I saw a confused face or someone gesturing at my outfit through the crowd, I shouted, *"Are you not entertained?!"* with an accompanying dramatic pose to illustrate who I was and watched the light bulbs go off (which happened more than a few times that night). Sure enough, the girl from the costume store found me in the crowd—the only issue was I was already dancing with a Disney princess. I thought I might be in trouble for inviting her and then being interested in someone else, but she had seemingly taken it in stride—and as the evening neared its end, all three of us snuck away to my bedroom.

Unfortunately, all the unbridled optimism wasn't meant to last.

The dot-com bubble began around 1995, and for years, everyone wanted a piece of the action. Companies were popping up left and right, and venture capitalists were hurling money at them, no matter how inane their product. Old companies were adding "dot com" to the ends of their names and seeing their stock valuations shoot through the roof, and that soaring energy continued all the way to its peak on Friday, March 10, 2000, when the NASDAQ Composite peaked at 5,048 points, up about 400 percent. The next day, the news broke in America that Japan had entered a recession. Overnight, everybody was thinking about how Japan's economic woes were sure to vibrate through the entire financial system and shake tech stocks. Suddenly, everybody wanted out. A massive sell-off ensued, investing sentiment flipped from frothy greed to white-knuckle fear, and Building Brokers was right in the middle of it.

Tensions were beginning to flare inside the company as well. One day, Richard called me asking for access to the company's capital account; because of his equity, in his view, he was entitled to access.

"Richard, respectfully, I can't do that," I replied.

"What, you don't trust me? What is this?" he asked, his voice rising.

"It's not that. I just don't think it's a good idea to have multiple people on the account," I said in return, trying to keep calm. "It's my responsibility to the investors, and I have to protect it." The topic came up a few more times in emails and calls, but the entire conversation had soured our relationship. After a few weeks, Richard announced that he was leaving the company. We bought back his equity and parted ways.

As predicted, tech stocks were being wiped out, and it was clear to every techie in New York that internet-related ventures were imploding. I was pushing Building Brokers on bankers and VCs as hard as I could, but I was leaving more and more meetings empty-handed. There was absolutely no appetite, and VC firms had practically sewn their pockets shut. To make matters worse, all the money we'd already secured—all $600,000 of it—was pretty much spent. It wasn't just Building Brokers that was going to shit; it seemed like the whole world was.

By 2001, Building Brokers hadn't generated any material revenue—not profit, mind you, *revenue*—and I gathered my staff to announce that we were closing shop. The actual announcement wasn't as emotionally difficult as I thought it would be, which surprised me somewhat. Since Richard had already left, it was just me, Eric, a few part-time employees and our interns. I tried to stay as optimistic as I could.

"All of you are fantastic, and your efforts have been so meaningful," I said to the room. "We did something great here, but unfortunately, there's no more money left to fund us. I have no doubt that all of these ideas will still be big in the future, but we have to shutter it for now." As unpleasant as the news was, it wasn't entirely unexpected. Even in the end, it felt like we were all in the same boat.

Harder than saying goodbye to everyone was actually moving out of the office. We didn't have any money for movers, so Eric and I dragged everything out by hand through countless long hallways down to the street while people watched. When we were done and down on street level, I looked up at the building. It was East 42nd Street, the Lincoln Building across from Grand Central. It was the same building where the Helmsleys had their offices, right on the top floor. They were still there; meanwhile, I was back on the sidewalk.

As much as I still loved the idea of modernizing real estate, bringing tech into an antiquated system, and revolutionizing commercial real estate, there was simply no energy left in the market. All the money was gone, and I was over-leveraged by about $50,000 after maxing out several credit cards, which seemed like a fortune. I wasn't just back to square one—I was worse off than when I started.

5

THE ART OF REBUILDING

With the tech sector collapsing around me, I wondered what I could have done differently to keep Building Brokers alive, if anything. Was the idea no good, or was it just ahead of its time? I got clarity from one of our competitors.

I'd been keeping tabs on a firm that offered services like our business and that had been backed by Goldman Sachs. When Building Brokers closed, we lost every bit of the $600,000 we raised and put into the business, plus what I'd put on credit cards to keep things afloat. That was nothing to scoff at, but our competitor had raised $50 *million* from Goldman for virtually the same product, and they had opened and shut in about six months. At Building Brokers, we'd kept the doors open and employees paid from 1999 to 2001 with way less money, which was some consolation. Whatever the takeaway was, my failures had been small enough, by comparison to seem like a success.

That $50 million figure shocked me and pulled me out of whatever shame spiral I was about to go down. The simple truth was my venture had launched during a ludicrous moment in tech and business, and I'd done the best I could, given the circumstances. Even so, my overwhelming feeling was disappointment.

The fall of Building Brokers was the truest failure I'd ever experienced. On top of it all, it was a risk I'd walked away from a profitable career in law to take—but my stomach was turning at the thought of going *back* to law after I'd gotten the taste of the life I actually wanted. I wanted to keep pushing into the real estate business, but I was out of gas and had no clear direction. I couldn't see my next move. It seemed that Eric could tell what I was thinking, because as we were moving out of our office on 42nd Street, he asked me.

"What's next then, Daniel?" He said as we were loading the last of the boxes into my car. "Do you have any applications out already? If you need some contacts, I'd be happy to lend a hand." As I slammed the trunk of my car, the answer came to me.

"Thanks, but no thanks, Eric," I replied. "I'm going to Club Med."

I didn't have much money or a trust fund to lean on, but I knew I had to take it easy for a little while. I was completely burnt out and was not motivated to return to law right away. All I really needed was to slow down and hopefully earn a little money while doing it. *I could interview for a job as a General Manager at Club Med and only stay for a season,* I thought. In my eyes, GMs were basically like adult camp counselors, and my background would be more than enough to qualify me for a seasonal position there. It would be working without working—meanwhile, I'd have time to get a tan on the beach, meet girls and plot my next moves. It symbolized everything other than having a purpose and a mission in life, which I wanted to try on for a little while— and even if my first instinct was to scramble for a way back onto a stable career path, I ignored it.

To get started, I did some research to make sure they were hiring. After that, I made a reservation at Club Med in Turks and Caicos for a week, packed a small bag and boarded my flight. As soon as the plane taxied and I made it through the airport, all I could see were powder-soft white sand beaches and an endless expanse of the bluest ocean all around me. This was definitely where I needed to be.

After getting settled in, I went down to the front desk to introduce myself and explain my intentions. We arranged for an interview the next day, and I pitched myself as best I could. From my experience at law firms, I explained, I had outstanding communication skills and plenty of client-facing experience. Finally, because I'd sailed with my father in my youth and was basically an unofficially certified instructor, I would also be great at teaching tourists how to sail.

The managers' faces brightened as I listed all my experience, and I was clearly on the cusp of getting the job. Still, their enthusiasm and mine were inversely proportional as they started explaining the specific responsibilities of the position. Rather than sleeping in, mingling with the resort's guests and sneaking in afternoon surf sessions, GMs were expected to be up early to greet everyone at breakfast and organize activities, among many other daily duties that didn't sound all that exciting. I realized I was selling myself to the staff just to do a watered-down version of what I really wanted to do: relax. I didn't want to teach tourists to sail. I wanted to be alone with my thoughts on a catamaran. I didn't want to work in paradise. I wanted to just *be* in paradise. I wanted my freedom again.

After the interview was over, I sat on the beach and let the water wash over my toes and the sun warm my skin. A few hours later, I went back to the front desk to withdraw my application and extended my stay indefinitely. As counterintuitive as it was, a total reset felt like the right move (even if it meant racking up more charges on my credit cards).

The next morning, I woke up early while the sun was rising and grabbed a catamaran to rip around a bit. While I was out, I watched the sky turn from purple to pink to a familiar bright blue as the sun came up. As the beach filled up with guests, I came in, ordered a beer and introduced myself to a graying retiree stretched out in a beach chair beside me.

"What brings you here, Daniel?" the man asked.

"Just taking a break from the city," I replied. I'd intended to keep it simple and not say more, but between the expectant look in the man's eyes and a little alcohol in my system, I couldn't help myself. "Actually, it's a little more than that. I started a business in New York City that I've been working on for years, and we just folded the company." Once I started, I couldn't stop, explaining in detail the difficulties of raising money, the partner who'd left the company, the difficult conversations I'd had with my employees—all of it. Without realizing it, I was purging years of stress onto a stranger. He listened patiently and sipped his own drink before replying.

"I used to come here with my wife Barbra before she passed," he said calmly. "We retired together, and this was our favorite place to stay." Before long, the man was telling me about his late wife, his children and how he'd spent his whole life building a business to provide for his family. We ordered another round of drinks—call it brunch—and at the end of it all, he tried offering me some advice.

"Nothing will bring Barbra back, and I've accepted that," he said. "Our time together was the greatest blessing of my life. For you, this business didn't work out—but you can always start another business. You have your whole life ahead of you." After some more idle chatter, we went our separate ways, but his words stuck with me. I always called interludes with strangers "going to camp" because they were brief moments in time with reciprocating strangers who knew very little about one another. Because of that, it was possible to dig very deeply into issues without any shame or restraint—you could share freely without any embedded prejudice or post-conversation shrapnel. I hadn't gone to camp much when I was younger, but these kinds of engagements were still ordinary course for me.

What my new friend had said was right. No matter how beaten down I was, Building Brokers wasn't the end of my story, and I hadn't lost anything I couldn't get back. With a shifted perspective, I decided I would forget the last year or so and would be as present as I could for the rest of my stay. For the following three weeks, I spent as much time in the sun as possible. I windsurfed and introduced myself to tourists and strangers. I was reminded of the carefree time I'd spent in Israel in college, which now felt so far away—it was an exceptional reminder that the best way to get clarity on something was to get some distance from it.

With my battery recharged, it was time to return to real

life. When Building Brokers closed, there were vendors in New York City who were owed money the company couldn't pay back (and wasn't legally required to). Even though I wasn't legally responsible for those debts, I still held myself personally responsible and didn't want to snub anyone or destroy good relationships. I'd only gone to Club Med because I figured taking a few more weeks to make good on what I owed wouldn't make much of a difference to vendors—but above all, I still intended to make things as right as possible.

When I got back to New York City, I started setting up meetings with everyone I owed and settled as many bills as I could. In my head, I heard my mom's voice: *Always be a mensch, Daniel.* I didn't intend to leave carnage in the wake of my failed business, so I did my best to live up to her advice.

I couldn't pay everything back immediately, but I made deals to pay what I could over an extended period of time— or else I settled for lower numbers that everyone could be happy with. It felt good being face to face with the people I'd done business with and to try to do right by them—but not all the conversations I had were entirely comfortable.

On my list of conciliatory meetings was one at Stroock & Stroock & Lavan with Joe Forstadt, a senior partner at the firm. Stroock was one of the powerful law firms in New York (and in the world, for that matter), so I steeled myself for what was coming. Upon walking into their lobby and shaking Joe's hand, I got to the meat of the conversation right away.

"I owe you money, I know," I said evenly, "and I want to do the right thing. Can I have a half-hour of your time?" Joe seemed a little surprised to see me in person. Building Brokers owed the firm somewhere between $30,000 and $40,000, money I certainly didn't have.

"These aren't ideal circumstances, and I don't have the money to settle my debt in full," I told him, maintaining eye contact the entire time. "Even so, I want to pay something back in good faith. I'm hoping we can settle for $10,000, which I can pay right away." That money meant a hell of a lot more to me to part with than it did to his firm, but I knew the settlement would mean the entire world for my reputation. It was something you couldn't put a price on.

"I appreciate you coming in for this," Joe said after our meeting was over. It was clear he respected me for engaging so directly, even if it was over bad news. "What's your plan now? Where do you go from here?"

"I just want to get back to work," I said frankly. "I want to get into real estate, make money and learn as much as I can." Joe nodded and smiled.

"If it would help, I could call Richard Maidman and put you two in touch?" He suggested. With those words, I felt my whole body reinflate. Richard H.M. Maidman was a New York City real estate investor, a prominent developer and a feared lawyer; he was also the owner and patriarch of the multi-generational Maidman real estate family, all of whom were lawyers (all the men were, at least).

"That would be terrific," I replied, trying to contain my enthusiasm.

"Perfect," Joe said, shaking my hand. "I'll set the meeting."

I spoke to Joe on a Monday, and my interview was scheduled that Wednesday at Maidman & Mittelman,

Richard's family-owned business that handled all legal business relating to their deals and properties. The office was in a gleaming high-rise between Park and Madison, one of the most prestigious and renowned parts of the city—but to my surprise, it wasn't on the higher floors. Instead, I followed signs into a cramped space in the basement of the skyscraper with harried secretaries and paralegals running around holding stacks of legal briefs. Upon descending the stairs, I was hit with an acrid, chemical smell that reminded me of fire and something else I couldn't place. As I later learned, it was the smell of burnt human hair from a salon that sat directly above the office. As I waded through the chaos to the back of the office, I was face-to-face with Richard Maidman.

"Nice to meet you, Daniel," he said while giving my hand a quick, firm shake. He looked over my resumé and asked me a few basic questions, but ultimately, I didn't get to spend much time qualifying myself. Instead, Richard told me everything there was to know about his family and the history of his business while I nodded appreciatively. I hadn't said much, but whatever I was doing was working because soon enough, he was pulling me out of my chair and walking me into the main office. "Why don't we go meet the boys?" he said.

He took me out into the din of the office floor once more to meet his son Mitchel and his nephew Gregory, both of whom were vibrating with nervous energy and seemed just as intense as Richard. After shaking hands with everyone and exchanging a few short pleasantries, Richard turned to me with finality.

"Daniel, you'll get great exposure here," he said. The

entire interview had taken about a half-hour, during which it seemed like I'd only spoken a few sentences.

"Absolutely, sir," I replied. "Does this mean I've got the job?" He furrowed his brow as if confused I'd even ask such a question.

"Yes, yes, let's see if you're a good fit," he said impatiently with a wave of his hand. "You start tomorrow." At the time, I couldn't believe how serendipitously I'd landed on my feet again. In retrospect, I now wonder if Joe from Stroock was secretly trying to exact revenge on me for coming up short.

As I learned quickly, Richard Maidman was no joke, and he ran a tough shop. His entire family worked at the office overseeing the family's investments, which included ongoing development and management of approximately 2,000 apartments around NYC (and to a lesser extent, a host of real estate holdings in New Haven, Connecticut). It was a firm with more complexity and integration than anything I'd done up to that point, connecting many dots involving law, real estate and investing. From the very get-go, Richard treated me no differently than he would've treated his son or nephew—in other words, with no mercy at all.

Richard was a drill sergeant in the office and very disciplined about getting every aspect of each deal perfectly right. He would chew out his underlings in front of the entire office (me included) and would make his lawyers go through 10 or more different iterations of a single document or brief until they suited him. Day in and day out, I heard lectures about how to do things better, how to be smarter and generally how to pull my head out of my own ass.

Every day in that office was a blizzard of documents,

transactions and fierce negotiations—and when they were busy, I was on the front lines of it all. To top it all, I was being sent into court regularly despite my inexperience.

"Lebensohn, we need you in court today for the Germaine case," Mitchel said, thrusting a file into my hands. As I scanned it, I saw it was a landlord-tenant dispute involving a woman named Gina Germaine.

"Sir, I haven't even had any motion practice yet," I started.

"I don't give a shit," he replied. "There are 10 or 15 cases on the docket today with different judges, so it's all hands on deck." I had never handled any real litigation before, but I had no choice but to fudge it and ask questions when I was there. Even so, I knew enough to know that landlord-tenant disputes could be a real shitshow, especially in New York City.

I went down to the courthouse to deal with a non-paying tenant who was staying in a building on West 43rd Street. When I got in the courtroom, I called out for Gina Germaine.

"That's me, honey!" a deep voice shouted back. I turned and saw a tall woman in a dress who had a man's physique. As it was my first time in court under any circumstances, the moment caught me off-guard—but inside, I had to laugh. I had been so self-conscious about how to comport myself in court, but something about that moment broke the tension and helped me get out of my head.

As surreal as it was, the effect of enduring so much daily mayhem was a raw, real-life master's degree that money couldn't buy. As I got more seasoned, the Maidmans sent me to court again and again. I was learning so much so fast that I was half afraid my brain would start hemorrhaging. For every office screaming match, wild emotional swing or out-of-control day in court, I remembered to breathe and reminded myself who I was. *I got through the collapse of my dream company in one piece*, I told myself. *I will make it through this as well.*

No matter how stressful it was, it was impossible not for part of you to be taken in by the close-knit and colorful energy of the office. Aside from all the legal business, everybody's personal business was flying around as well. Every day there were new details about feuds within the family or rumors about who on the office team was having their own life drama. It was a strange bazaar for airing everything personal and inappropriate. All the secretaries were streetwise ladies who were constantly shouting at the Maidmans, and the family gave as good as they got, shouting right back. The family lived up to their image—they were every inch the remote and unrelatable tycoons of New York real estate everyone said they were.

One morning, I was supposed to be doing diligence on a country club near the Financial District. My power had gone out the night before, so my alarm didn't wake me up, and I slept in later than I usually would—when I awoke, it was around 8:30 am. In a little less than 20 minutes, I quickly got dressed and grabbed my bike to go to work when my phone rang. It was my friend and brother Yaniv Noach from Israel.

"Are you safe?" he asked in a panicked voice in Hebrew as I picked up the phone. I was confused.

"Yes, I'm fine," I replied. "Why do you ask?"

"Turn on your TV," he replied. As I did so, I saw that the Twin Towers in the Financial District were on with smoke billowing out of the North Tower. The anchor was explaining that a plane had flown into the tower at 8:46 am, and his tone was confused—had it been a tragic accident? Was it intentional? I stood stunned, watching the TV and talking to Yaniv, when a second plane flew into the South Tower at 9:02 am. It was no accident. The city was under attack.

I rode my bike to work in shock as smoke filled the air on the south side of the island and everything ground to a stop. Subways were stuck on their tracks, roads were closing and traffic was frozen with police deployed everywhere. The fear in the air was one everyone shared; nobody knew whether the attacks would continue all day, all over the city.

When I finally arrived at the office, one of the administrators was in hysterics. She had survived World War II as a child in Paris, and that morning's experience was bringing back painful memories that had sent her over the edge. The atmosphere was frenzied—but meanwhile, Richard Maidman was emanating an off-kilter energy, calmly telling everyone to get to their desks and back to work.

The morning and the weeks that followed shocked the entire city. Later on, I biked down to the scene of the towers with friends to try and volunteer at the attack site, though we were waved away by police and firefighters. I replayed the fact that my alarm hadn't gone off that morning countless times. Above all, the magnitude of the event gave me a new perspective on what I had thought were harsh times in the basement of the Maidman office. Now, all I could see was how amazing normal life in the city was and how easy it was to take for granted. Amidst so much tragedy, being near someone like Richard Maidman was surreal—the amount of discipline and removal he had to keep everyone moving forward and focused on work in the present was difficult to understand.

Later that year, the Maidmans were working on acquiring properties at 554 3rd Avenue, and I was assigned to finalize the land assemblages, work on the master lease and do whatever else they needed me to do. It was a deal with some interesting complications. The Maidmans had plans to build a 32-story skyscraper on their lot but to get the squarest footage out of it, they wanted the building to be wider in the middle than it was at the base. They planned to accomplish that by cantilevering the upper floors, but it meant that they would have to build in the airspace above one or more of the buildings around it (or else would have to buy adjacent lots to make sure they could construct the way they wanted to). Though I was familiar with the concept of air rights from law school, it would be my first real experience researching and negotiating them—and the same was true of the ZLDAs we would have to pull (Zoning Lot Development Agreements).

Although having a building on 3rd Avenue offered the Maidmans a ton of value, leasing out a building that large presented a real challenge. The Maidmans would need to take out a large loan for approximately 70 percent of the total cost of the building. In addition to securing a loan that large, it was also a race to market; even if a developer had a brilliant idea, missing the market spelled near-inevitable doom and failure, no matter how sharp the developer. In many cases, personal guarantees accompanied these leveraged positions, meaning liability extended beyond just losing the property itself—it meant that if you went underwater, the lender could come after your personal assets to recoup their losses.

To finance the deal, Mitchel Maidman and his wife Arlene had an idea to network with some Israeli investors she knew who had a relationship with Marriott. Marriott needed a new location for hotel rooms, and this new building would be a perfect fit. Their solution was to split the building into a massive, long-term lease Marriott would control, plus condos on top that the Maidmans would sell out as an additional revenue stream. While getting a bank to loan millions for a building with no tenants in it was one thing, bringing them the same deal with Marriott attached in a 30-year lease suddenly made it much more attractive—they were a tenant with incredible credit that automatically took up 25 of the 32 stories and thus provided a nearly guaranteed income stream.

"We're going to finance this on the heels of the Marriott lease," Mitchel told me, "and we'll have a coupon for the next 30 years." The beauty, as he explained, was that when the lease expired, the Maidmans would have control over the entire building despite only putting a nominal amount of their own money into it up front. It was a long-term trade where most of the value got unlocked at the end, and it was designed to set the family up for generations to come. In all, it must've been a $150 million project.

With the Marriott lease, air rights and zoning negotiated, the Maidmans put me in touch with CIBC bank to firm up a loan. It was how I met Mike Wadler, a senior-level banker who was in charge of underwriting the financing on the deal. When the time came, Mitchel, Gregory and I were in the same room negotiating with a panel of senior-level bankers, one of whom was Mike. At the Maidmans, it wasn't uncommon for major banks to send high-level representatives to our office for aggressive negotiations over complex deals. What was uncommon, however, was for those senior executives to acknowledge the existence of a junior lawyer like me who they perceived as below their paygrade. Fortunately, Mike was not your usual senior-level banker.

Over the next year or so, while we were closing the deal, Mike was generous enough to take me out to lunch from time to time. As I got to know him, I saw that he had something of a conservative dad's mentality. He was 15 years my senior and had been with large institutions his whole life. He embraced a company man mindset, but he still had incredible knowledge and insights from his long career to boot.

"I'm sure they're chewing you up over there, Danny," he said, "but the experience you're getting is priceless. Your ambitions of owning and developing real estate on your own —do it! But remember that you can grow and expand without cutting your legs off or giving up your foundation. It doesn't have to be one or the other."

———

After a few more lunches with Mike, I'd started internalizing his advice and was doing my best to get into the flow of the work—even if my bosses weren't letting up very much. I had surer footing in court and was doing fiercer negotiations, taking more and more off the senior partners' plate. Some days I was practicing law, some days I was closing real estate business deals with the Maidmans, and sometimes I was driving Richard out to his mansion on Long Island.

Even if it was chaotic, I considered the personal errands a perk—one of the advantages of driving Richard to his mansion on the weekends was that I could keep his 1995 Country Range Rover until I had to pick him up again, which came in handy since I didn't have a car at the time. After I dropped him off, I would drive to the Hamptons. In the summers, Kurt and I split a share house that Ari and David visited to hang out and party—and when I pulled up in that car, I felt like a rock star. It was like going on high school joyrides all over again.

After getting to know the Maidman family a little better, it was clear that each of them was brilliant in their own way. It was also clear that they were overlooking things, letting personal foibles get in the way of business and leaving a lot of money on the table. They were detail-oriented and painstaking about every document and detail, focusing on any and every minute aspect rather than looking up to see the big picture. They insisted on doing everything themselves. When I worked with my clients, I did my best to look behind the contracts to give my own insights into their business and help them understand the deals better. They liked how engaged I was, and time and time again, I tried to do the same for the Maidmans.

In my humble view, the family had three generations' worth of real estate business and credibility that they weren't putting to good use—why not use the Maidman name to grow a multibillion-dollar fund? Why not offload the legal end of the business somewhere else and grow? If they didn't want to do that, why not at least compartmentalize some of the in-house divisions and compound wealth? Take the operation and 10X it! I raised my perspective a few times, but at the end of the day, I was an employee with big eyes. Usually, the response was the same.

"Daniel, I can't do this right now," Mitchel would say. "Do you see how many files I have here? Get the fuck out of my office." To their credit, it was an open forum at their office—I could say my piece and get my head cut off, but it ended there.

No matter what anyone had to say, the Maidmans had their own way of doing things. Because they were a wealthy family with a history in business, they had a big cushion and a different mindset. It wasn't about streamlining and expanding for them; it was about maintaining the power they already had and avoiding unnecessary risks. Meanwhile, I was taking mental notes about how I would run my own affairs in the future—and when I would be able to go out on my own.

6

CLOSING THE FIRST DEAL

Though Mike's advice was still ringing in my ears, I was more focused on the implications of the second part of it: I didn't have to give up my foundation (and my income) to do the things I really wanted to do. In my case, it meant being more entrepreneurial and putting together my own deals—and my first big opportunity to do so was somewhat unexpected.

At a business mixer, I bumped into a guy named Donald Trooien, who I had met a few times before. When we were still dating, Jackie had introduced Don and me, saying that we should do business together. When I found out that Don and Jackie had dated, I wasn't too keen on the idea. Regardless, now that I was single, it seemed like it couldn't hurt if Don and I had a conversation.

As I soon realized, Jackie had been right to try and set us up before—Don was a very nice guy, and we hit it off almost immediately. His company's name was Troystar, and it mainly dealt with sourcing, building, leasing, buying and selling billboards in and around New York City.

"I run into a lot of problems with landlords," he said with a groan. "I could really use the help of a smart attorney, and it seems like we would be a good fit. I think I'll have a lot of work for you." Anybody who frequently found themselves in trouble with landlords was an ideal client for a real estate lawyer, so after thinking it over, we shook hands. Though I'd "found" him as a client, I brought his case files through Maidman & Mittelman as per the proper procedure—and because I'd brought in new work, I got a commission on top of whatever billable hours I might accrue doing work for him.

The more we worked together, the closer Don and I grew, and the more questions I asked him about how he ran his business. From what I could tell, it was a very interesting proposition. While there was plenty of money to be made in real estate, billboards seemed to function quite a bit differently as an asset. In a place like New York City with strict zoning laws and a lot of development, they were more like a public utility than a regular piece of property. If you controlled a billboard, you could rent it out to a big company on a long-term lease and collect a huge monthly check. It sounded like a perfect first venture to help set me up on my own, so in 2003, I approached Don about teaming up together in a new way.

"If you ever want to partner on one of these sign investments, let me know," I told him. "I can invest, do the legal work for free, and I'm good on my feet. I'd love to be your guy." Though he didn't seem uninterested, I wasn't sure anything would come of it or if he was even interested in cutting anyone in on his business. Even so, he said he would get back to me. Later on, he came back to me with a proposal on a new billboard deal.

"I have a good one for you to get started on," Don told me one day. "I need a capital partner." After looking over the details more closely, it seemed he wanted me to do legal work and invest a 10 percent interest on a sign while he kept the other 90 percent. I frowned—what I'd had in mind was an equal partnership, not to be taken advantage of.

"I appreciate the offer, Don," I replied not impolitely, "but I don't think the balance is right here. Let me know when you want to be full 50-50 partners, and we can talk again." Again, I thought a second offer might never come— but to my surprise, he approached me with new terms on another deal a few months later.

"I have these two leases on parking lots in Chelsea on 23rd and 10th and 28th and 10th," he told me. "They're both near the old High Line train tracks, and they're owned by a guy named David, who secured them from a landlord named Gary Spindler. After we buy them from David for $50,000, we can put up billboards. I know a contractor who can build the first sign all in for $180,000, hard and soft costs, and we'll be in business," Don told me. "What do you say?"

As Don explained, he and I would divide the costs and the profits evenly. It was exactly the kind of deal I wanted, but I knew I would have to have it run by the Maidman family for clearance. To my pleasant surprise, however, they were completely fine with it.

"Sounds interesting," Mitchel said without looking up from the papers in front of him. "You're interested in doing that? Billboards?"

"It seems like a good opportunity," I offered weakly. Mitchel nodded and shrugged.

"Have fun, then," he replied.

————

From knowing Don's business inside and out, it was clear that billboards could be a very profitable investment. All the same, they required a lot of special permits and rights to build (which I already knew from knowing Don's business inside and out)—and the money we had to put up seemed like a lot to sink into the *prospect* of building and renting one.

Practicing law tends to make one more pessimistic and thus more risk-averse, but the back-of-the-napkin math made sense: the lease costs would be about $2,500 a month, and there would be construction to pay back, but I would still have good income coming in to cover me from working at the Maidmans—and when the sign was up, we could lease it out and collect income there as well. The finished asset would be worth at least $12,500 a month in revenue, even during a bad month. At an occupancy of 10 months a year and approximately $12,500 per month or $125,000 in revenue per year, the baseline returns were shaping up to be phenomenal. It made sense, so I was ready to jump in.

To keep everything in good financial order, I started a company called Wilder Realty, borrowing from an old DBA my dad used years prior (as a tribute to my family's initials— W for my dad, Walter; IL for Ilana and Lisa, my mom and sister; D for Daniel and ER for "earning rent"). Given my past entrepreneurial endeavors and my multi-faceted experience at the Maidmans, I was confident Don and I could creatively finance the deal. We would have to because neither of us had $180,000 to spend. It seemed like a monumental sum of capital at the time, but the promise of eventual rewards was greater than my fear of filling the cost gap.

Our first step was to pay an engineer Don knew named Chabon to draw up the plans for putting in the sign. After that, we needed to pay a deposit with the contractor, a tough guy named Teddy, to get him to pull permits and start building. From the very beginning, it was hard finding regular money to pay Teddy, which was causing problems.

"I need the money if you want me to put this project together!" he would shout at us. "If you can't come up with it, I'll go to the landlord myself and keep this project going without you."

"Teddy," I said, "We're good for the money; we just need a little time. As soon as the sign is built, the checks will start rolling in, and we'll all get paid." No matter what we said, he didn't want to hear it. He wanted cash in his hand right away.

I figured I might need some help with the Teddy situation, so I started brainstorming. I was still practicing law, and one of the clients I'd helped with some difficult litigation was in the demolition business. He was a big guy named Peter who was a tough and intimidating person with deep connections in New York (though behind the scenes, I knew him as a gentle giant). I told him a bit about my problem with Teddy, and he offered to jump in right away.

"What do you want me to do, Daniel?" he asked. "Do you want me to talk to him?"

"No, you don't have to talk to him," I said. "But maybe you could come sit in a meeting with me and pretend to be my partner?" He agreed right away, and I figured with him by my side, I could do one final negotiation with Teddy for a payment plan he would have to stick to once and for all.

Later that week, I told the Maidmans I needed to use one of their conference rooms and invited Teddy and Peter in for the meeting. As soon as Teddy sat down, he couldn't help but notice my silent, hulking friend sitting beside me. "Who is this guy?" Teddy asked irritably.

"He's a friend of mine," I said casually. "He's sitting in." After that, I launched into the terms of the payment plan. Don and I would pay Teddy $15,000 in monthly installments until the sign was finished, and we would aggressively pay off the rest of the debt over time from sign revenue. Without a doubt, Teddy was not pleased with the terms of the deal—but he also didn't want to learn more about my relationship with Peter. After that meeting, he agreed to the terms, and our project was smoothly underway again.

For the next several months, delays and all, Don and I scraped together $2,500 a month to pay the landlord, Gary, on top of the money we needed to pay Teddy to keep him building. Before and after work, in the middle of winter, I would walk down to the construction site wearing my suit and thin leather shoes, freezing my ass off as I watched the project come to fruition. Even though I was completely harried between working full-time and trying to get this project off the ground, it was comforting to know that I had money coming in and that I hadn't needed to go out entirely on my own to start materializing my entrepreneurial dreams. Still, I needed my risk to pay off; no matter how you looked at it, I was into these billboards for a lot of money.

Before construction was finished, Don heard that The

Container Store was coming to New York City and to Manhattan specifically. "To build awareness for their brand and their business, they're definitely going to have a big advertising budget," Don said. "What if we pitched them on leasing our sign? It's in a prime location for them—we're aimed directly at their demographic."

It was as good an idea as any other we had, so he reached out to their ad agent and tried to strike up a deal for a 12-month lease. They wouldn't agree to that up front, but they did agree to six months—and later, they agreed to keep re-renting. We were still heavily leveraged on the construction, but just a month after inking the deal, Don and I were collecting approximately $18,000 a month in revenue on the sign and splitting it evenly. It was more than I had ever made in a month from practicing law.

Seeing those numbers on that first little check was a complete paradigm shift materializing. I realized I could take on risk up front and do a lot of work all at once and then collect checks in perpetuity. The next steps were simple: we would apply all the revenue, less the lease costs, to paying off Teddy until our debts were cleared. After that, we would keep collecting passive income—and no matter how busy I was, I planned to rinse and repeat.

7

A NEW LEASE ON LIFE AND BUSINESS

As I got more experienced, I got into a rhythm at the Maid-mans of spending more and more time in New Haven. Multiple times a week, I drove up to check up on their business endeavors in the area, whether because the firm was trying to buy out tenants or renters were suing over lead-based paint. As a result of all the time I was spending in the area, I was getting to know the local team in New Haven, including Elmer Rivera.

Elmer was a real estate manager for the Maidmans' New Haven properties, whereas I was their go-to asset manager from the New York side. Elmer was a short, unassuming man with a mustache, and he was both resourceful and quick on his feet in the area. He knew all the tenants well and had relationships with all the important local real estate figures. Though we came from different backgrounds, Elmer had a scrappiness and latent ambition about him that I had to respect, and we'd started to develop a rapport.

The final leg of our New Haven triangle was Scott

Hurwitz, counsel for the Maidmans who represented their work and local interests in New Haven. Because the Maidmans weren't particularly active about their interests outside the city, they had guys like Elmer, myself and Scott to deal with smaller headaches. Scott was an established lawyer and real estate investor who shared a practice with his father, a local estate lawyer. Our conversations were meant to be limited to legal details and case-specific frustrations, but Scott's sharp, business-minded demeanor gradually gave way to a gentle exchange of ideas about life and dreams for the future (and some good-natured chuckles over the Maidmans' signature holiday cards, which had the patriarch and matriarch dressed up as superheroes and famous villains and were infamous in New York City circles).

As the demands of work got more intense, Kurt and I were hitting the town as much as we could after work to relieve workday stress, and hopefully, find some romance. Kurt had recently had a modest exit from his own company and was feeling a bit angsty at the time. Both of us were more than in the mood to blow off steam. Amid all my social adventures, I went on a group blind date at The Ginger Man. It was organized by a friend of David Zarabi's, and I invited my whole entourage. I had a few drinks and mingled with the crowd, but there was one woman across the room with whom I kept making eye contact. Eventually, she came up to me and introduced herself.

"They said you were Israeli," she said plainly. "You're not Israeli." I laughed—my strategy of playing it cool had worked. She told me her name was Rachel, and right away, we had chemistry. She had great energy, and we started talking about our jobs, our dreams, our likes and our dislikes. After that, the conversation took a turn into a darker place.

"A lot of who I am today is because of what happened to me when I was a little girl," she said. "I lost my father when I was very young. I had to be independent very early on." I was moved that we already had a deep enough connection that she felt comfortable sharing that with me—and I felt myself opening up.

"My family experienced a serious loss as well," I said quietly. "I don't tell many people this, but my sister Tammy died when I was very young. Like you said, it has had a seismic impact on our family." The more we talked, it was clear there was a much more profound connection between us than just basic flirtation. With the chemistry we had established, we shared a kiss at the bar that was fully recip- rocated.

"You're pretty proud of yourself, aren't you?" she said. I just smiled. At the end of the night, I was flagging down a cab for Rachel when I leaned in for a kiss. As it was pulling up, I realized we had not yet exchanged numbers.

"So, I guess we will get in touch with smoke signals, then?" I said. She smirked and pulled out a pen and paper to pass me her phone number before the cab drove off. When that leg of the night was over, I was beyond ener- gized and met back up with my buddy for a scotch at a dive bar. After that was over, I went to Ari's apartment to have another scotch and explained what had happened. After talking non-stop about Rachel, I noticed Ari was smiling.

"I've never seen you like this, Daniel," Ari said. "You really think this girl is special."

I nodded. "I think I just met the girl I'm going to marry, Ari," I replied.

On our first real date, I used Richard Maidman's season tickets to take Rachel to the New York Philharmonic, and after that, we ate dinner at Rosa Mexicano across from Lincoln Center. While it was already a special night, what made it even better was a cute blonde named Ronnie, who I used to date, saw me and came over to our table to say hello. I could not have planned it any better—there was nothing better for my chances with Rachel than getting a solid endorsement from another woman at a critical moment.

Soon enough, I was moving out of my old apartment and into a new one with Rachel. Around the same time, Kurt met a new girl that he was taken with named Marcie, and they started dating as well. The beauty of it was that Kurt and Marcie moved into a new apartment right across the street from Rachel and me, which meant that we were always going on double dates and spending time together as couples.

In addition to my legal work, Don and I were doing more and more sign deals around the city, and I was angling to become a billboard tycoon. At the peak of our ventures together, we had signs on the Long Island Expressway near the Midtown Tunnel and another one in Inwood. It meant we were clearing $300,000 or more a year! I was enjoying all the extra income, but I was still not pushing nearly as hard as I could have. Instead, I was spending the new money and extra time I had enjoying life in the city with Rachel.

As great as the sign business was, it was firmly in the "unsexy" bucket of investments. From an early age, what Ari, Kurt, David and I had been really passionate about was actual real estate deals—multi-family homes that real families lived in and which we could rent out. The immigrant business mindset our fathers had drilled into us was still lingering, and I wasn't sure I wanted to be known only as the billboard guy. I wanted to get started in multi-families in earnest, but I didn't want to give up the billboard income stream either. To work the situation out, I approached Don with a proposal.

"Listen, Don," I said. "I have ambitions to start my own real estate business, and I'm ready to get started, but I know we have a great thing going here. You know this business, and I know real estate inside and out. What if we partnered up in a strategic alliance?" It was an idea I'd gotten from the Maidmans. Richard had approached another businessman who owned parking lots all around the city, and he'd struck a deal with him: in exchange for 10 percent of the man's profits from parking lots, Richard would give him 10 percent of the family's profits from real estate—and on either side of the equation, both parties had the right to go in on or pass on any deal. They were great terms that opened the door to a ton of additional income while letting each partner focus on what they knew best. But Don wasn't interested.

"That doesn't sound appealing to me," Don said. "You're welcome to do whatever you have to do, but I'm satisfied with this business. I want to keep growing it and keep the equity. Tell you what—even though I'm not interested, if you find any other signs we could work on together in the future, let's do it." The conversation hadn't gone the way I wanted. Beyond being business partners, Don and I were good friends. I knew I could grow something great in real estate, and his refusal to team up with me felt like he didn't have confidence in my abilities. It felt personal—so in my immaturity, I made it personal.

I considered myself a free agent, meaning I could do whatever I wanted around the city—including sign deals that I brought in and closed on my own. Since I still felt angry from the partnership that hadn't worked out, I went looking for the biggest possible sign deal I could take down on my own and found it in Manhattan. It was a 6,500-square-foot sign on the side of the Guggenheim Museum's storage facility on the West Side Highway, a huge, unmarked building that served as storage for incalculable precious artworks. I got control of it by calling the Guggenheim's head of real estate relentlessly and asking him about it and ultimately signed a 10-year lease with them. After leasing it from the Guggenheim, I subleased it for $12,500 per month to one of Don's competitors, a larger player in the New York metro area by the name of Van Wagner. Not long after, I got a call from Don.

"How could you do that?!" he shouted into the phone—I'd never heard him so pissed before. "I thought we had a deal!"

"What are you talking about?" I shot back. "I offered you a deal, and you said no! Your deal is I'm restricted on signs, but you're not? That's bullshit!" After spewing at each other some more, it seemed clear we weren't going to be able to co-operate on the signs we currently had in our portfolio together. Although we talked through our disagreement, both of our egos were hurt. Finally, I sold the LIE signs for $250,000 to the landlord because he was selling the building and he needed the signs unencumbered, and we ended up splitting the trade. After that, we split the signs we'd taken on together as evenly and amicably as possible and agreed to go our own separate ways.

I still loved the sign business, but the entire experience made me want to clear my plate of all the management headaches and put my focus on something else. Like I'd done with the Guggenheim deal, I decided to license the remaining signs I had—about half a dozen at that time—out to others who would source advertisers and pay me a base rent and some percentage of revenue, eliminating virtually all my time commitment. It would mean less net revenue but much more free time. I was taking all the unpleasantness that had occurred as a sign that it was time to push into real estate and to get a big deal done on my own. I figured shaking off some of my duller responsibilities would unlock my ability to hunt for better investments. Despite my best efforts, however, I wasn't finding many.

Soon after, a friend of mine from law school named Marc sent me a setup about the Sands Hotel and Casino on the Las Vegas Strip—it was in distress, and it seemed that either the ownership or the lender was trying to liquidate the asset. Right away, I was fixated on it—it was exactly the kind of real estate deal I really wanted to be working on. Since I was buzzing off the strength of how I had restructured my billboard business, my confidence that I could pull something together to close was at an all-time high. I brainstormed about which wealthy real estate investors I might call and sketched out some preliminary plans of what I would do with the space. After all that, I called David Zarabi to tell him my plans.

"I'm thinking about trying to buy the Sands Hotel in Las Vegas," I told David. As I explained to him, the billboard score had been huge, but it was something I'd done using someone else's connections to get started. It was a business model Don had already established, and it wasn't really the kind of real estate I was most interested in anyway. There wasn't much art, history or culture in it. I needed to see if I could do a big deal again—but by myself, my way.

"Daniel," David said, "Why are you trying to do a mega-deal right away? You're talking about getting started here. Why not just get a smaller deal done and stop looking at these massive deals?" He may have deflated my enthusiasm, but he also made me stop and think. I wanted redemption from the failed partnership with Don, and I wanted to get another win on the level of Building Brokers again. No matter how great this new passive income stream was, my appetite was growing beyond my station. My friend Ian's father had once told me about people who "didn't match their wishbone with backbone." It occurred to me that I was doing the exact same thing. I was caught up in "wishbone thinking," but it didn't matter if I couldn't meet it with follow-through and experience.

David was right. I had time to gain momentum first with a small deal—any deal. I would humble myself, find a modest deal I could deliver on my own and actually get it done. I spread the word at the office and to some of my clients that I was looking for an investment opportunity. As the ultimate eyes on the ground in New Haven, where properties were relatively cheap compared to New York, it was Elmer who brought me my opportunity.

"There's a couple living at 66 Chapel Street, and they're getting foreclosed," Elmer told me one day. "It's a modest four-family home, priced at $70,000." He told me more about the layout, the surrounding area and some of what it would take to put the deal together. Anyone in the business knew that the real estate in New Haven was uneven, and a lot of it looked terrible upon a surface glance—in many places, one block would be rough while the next one looked great. There was a lot of gang activity and crime, and many of the properties were beat up. Even so, 66 Chapel Street looked exciting as hell to me—even if it was a real piece of dreck (as we say in Yiddish).

Yale was only a mile away, and there was sure to be a rotating crop of well-to-do college students who would fill the house for years to come if it were fixed up the right way. I hadn't even seen the place yet, but just like my billboard deals, my gut told me there was something there. "I'm going to send you a binding letter of intent to present to the couple that owns it," I said to Elmer. "Let's get this locked up immediately."

Soon after, I went to the Maidmans to get their blessing to make a move in the area—and their blessing to use one of their lawyers. Once again, they approved, and I called Scott to tell him the news.

"Scott, I want to have you represent me in the deal," I said. During our mutual tenure working for the Maidmans, Scott had become so much more to me than a business colleague. Between our usual commentary about people we worked with and the daily stresses of the job, we also spoke more broadly about life, business and the future. He had become a confidant and dear friend who I'd grown to trust—and all this even though we had never met in person.

"Hey, if the Maidmans give their blessing, I'm game,"

Scott replied. I couldn't see his face, but I could sense him smiling on the other end of the phone.

After I faxed Scott all the legal documents and other necessities, I drove to New Haven one weekend to look at the property in person. Though it was rough around the edges, I prided myself on having seen value somewhere nobody else had yet. Like the billboard deal, the simple math on the house made sense—and to add to that, the couple selling it were over their skis on the place and wanted to move out of the state. All those things added up were good indicators of an anxious seller, which was clearly a good buying opportunity.

It would cost about $75,000 to get things rolling. I didn't have the cash to shoulder all that risk myself, so once again, I had to get creative. *How can I get this deal done?* I wondered. *I could try to finance the property, sure, but it's in foreclosure.* It seemed too complicated. I needed something that was as simple as possible, so I tried to apply my legal mind to find an angle that would benefit everyone.

The situation was that this soon-to-be evicted couple owned the home I was interested in, and they weren't making their mortgage payments. That meant that their lender was out a lot of money—and this was a private lender rather than a bank, so the pain of being out that money was probably much more substantial. The reality was I didn't have all the cash to put in at once, but I did have enough to partially pay down the mortgage payments the lender wasn't getting, at least temporarily. If I got the lender to extend the mortgage and trust me to pay it, it would be the best outcome for everyone involved. He was under no legal obligation to do that, of course, but I had to give it a shot.

For starters, I called the attorney representing the lender. "Is it possible to extend the terms of the mortgage for 12 months?" I asked.

"That's not something my client is interested in," he replied sternly. It was a short phone call.

Next, I conferred with Scott to see if he thought what I was proposing was possible.

"It can't hurt to ask," he said. I ran it by Elmer as well, figuring he might have a little more sway in the situation since he knew the people involved more personally.

"There's no way," Elmer said. "Why would he do that? He doesn't know you, and there's no advantage for him. You need to find another way."

I had already thought it through and knew this *was* the best way—even if some could not see the elegance and simplicity of what I was proposing. They didn't know the drive I had. I knew if I made a good sales pitch, I could close the deal myself.

"Can you give me the lender's phone number?" I asked Scott.

When I finally connected with the lender, I set into my sales pitch. "I want to close this deal, but it needs to make financial sense for everyone involved," I said. "You're already in the process of foreclosure. You're not getting paid, and the deed is coming into my hands, subject to your mortgage and a lien on the property—and that's all well and good, but actually extracting the money out of that arrangement is going to take a lot of time, and you and I both know that."

There was silence on the other end of the line. Not hearing a no, I continued:

"The good news is I'm an upright guy who's good for the

money and who can make your payments, but I need a little cooperation as everything changes hands," I said carefully. "What I propose is that you stop all your legal proceedings and agree to carry the mortgage for another 12 months. We'll skip all the complexity and the waiting around. I'll give you $5,000 immediately once we close this deal, and I'll make your payments going forward. Even if you don't know me, there's not much downside for you here—best case is I start putting money back in your pocket right away; worst case is you foreclose on me, take the property back and you're in the same situation you are now—even better, really, because I'll be fixing up the property too. What do you say?"

He thought about it for a minute. Despite every no I'd gotten leading up to the conversation, I finally got the yes I'd been looking for.

8

MISADVENTURES IN NEW HAVEN

With Scott's legal acumen, Elmer and I closed on the title for the four-family for $62,500, and with that, Elmer and I put up $20,000 in equity (with me putting up the lion's share). I dropped about $300 worth of paint into the place and hired people to clean it up. We didn't really renovate it—it was more like putting lipstick on a pig, but it was enough. Soon after, the property was ready to go on the market again.

After showing it around, we sold it for $125,000—clearing nearly a 275 percent profit on our investment! After mortgage costs and other expenses, it meant walking away with my money back and about $55,000 in profit for just six months of nominal work. It wasn't a fortune, but it seemed like a treasure trove to me at the time—especially because I was making $85,000 as a lawyer working six to seven days a week for an entire year.

Flipping that four-family home was a turbo booster for my confidence. I felt like I'd been scraping sticks together for years, and I finally had a roaring fire in front of me. It was enough to push me into making the next big step. The time had finally come to leave Maidman & Mittelman to pursue more of my own investments. It was shortly after that realization that a headhunter reached out to me.

"There's a boutique firm named Hartman & Craven, and they're looking for a new associate," he said. "If you're interested, I can set up an interview." I had heard of Hartman & Craven before—they were a pedigreed shop not too far away from the Maidman office, and the properties and deals they were working on seemed a little more interesting. As a bonus, they were offering about $50,000 more per year in compensation. In thinking it through, I was reminded of Mike Wadler's advice. I hadn't been making much money at the Maidmans, but Hartman & Craven offered more compensation and could be a great base for entrepreneurial ventures. My feeling was I'd be able to work on bigger deals and continue to grow my network and relationships while still pursuing my own investments. After a short call, I agreed to an interview.

That first interview was with the firm's managing partner, Steve O'Connell. After I walked through my resumé and explained my qualifications, the room went quiet.

"You seem very entrepreneurial," Steve said quietly. "Though you have the qualifications, we're looking for someone who is going to stick around and build the firm with us. I'm a bit concerned that's not what you're looking for here." He was right, of course, but I still wanted the job for the time being. I saw their firm as a place where I could meaningfully contribute while also pursuing my broader dreams but also didn't want to be disingenuous in my response.

"Mr. O'Connell," I replied, "I'm very interested in building my CV, getting experience at this kind of boutique shop and helping on the esteemed deals you work on here at Hartman & Craven. I believe I'd be a great asset to the team. I'd love to help be part of your firm and build your business. I am entrepreneurially minded without question, but I hope to use it to contribute to the firm's success." Apparently, that was enough from me. Despite his initial instincts, the rest of the interview went well, and he offered me the position.

When I went to give my notice, I walked into Richard's office and announced my plans to leave the firm. Mitchel was standing beside him when I broke the news, and I saw his face sour. Though I'd been bracing myself for their reaction, Richard surprised me by taking it in stride.

"Good for you, Daniel," he said proudly.

In the few weeks I had left at the firm, Mitchel was none too pleased—but the respect level from Richard had shot through the roof. Our rapport had grown exponentially, and I could understand why. Ultimately, Richard was an old-school gentleman at heart. He admired my tenacity and respected my departure. Even though his firm had turned into a stable business over the years, it hadn't started that way—and it was easy for him to admire someone with enough drive to go after their dreams.

Right away, I could tell Hartman & Craven was going to be different than working at Maidman & Mittelman. From day one, I had two or three times as many direct bosses, and though they weren't as loud or abrupt as the Maidman family, they were certainly strange birds with sharp tongues and demanding appetites. One partner always mumbled to himself and walked around sucking an unlit pipe. Another senior partner would call you in for a meeting, never make eye contact with you and just look past you while tapping his head.

In all, the idiosyncrasies were humorous and added some levity to a demanding job with a heavy caseload. I respected many of the lawyers at the firm tremendously, and their entire operation felt so polished. The money they were offering was also great, so I wanted to do more than enough to impress them. It was a huge opportunity to learn and grow, so I was determined to crush it.

At any given time at Hartman & Craven, I had dozens of open files on closings, leases and other real estate dealings. Like it had been at the Maidmans, it was ostensibly okay to pursue my own investments outside the firm if I funneled the legal work through them—but all the same, I had to be a bit more discreet than I had been before. While Maidman & Mittelman had an underlying entrepreneurial mindset that they encouraged in their own employees, Hartman & Craven were more institutionally minded. From their view, their firm existed to do legal work for other clients, not for themselves. It was made clear when I approached Steve, who had since become a buddy of mine, to see if he'd invest in a deal I was looking at.

"I don't think that's appropriate, Daniel," he said, almost aghast.

"Why not?" I asked. He shook his head and said it just wasn't how things were done before walking away. From my perspective, the partners at Hartman & Craven knew all about real estate, so why wouldn't they also invest in what they knew? It was another example of my resistance to conventionality brushing up against the restrictive culture of the legal world. More pointedly, some of the partners were not too interested in seeing an associate sprout wings too soon.

I wanted to do more house flips like I'd done with Elmer as a stepping stone to some of my bigger goals. It had been about seven months since we'd done one, and I didn't know why he hadn't called to take on another. I knew Elmer was a scrapper and had an entrepreneurial mindset like me, and we'd done a good job together on the first four-family deal. He had been my junior partner in that first deal, and he'd made money. I figured I would give him another call myself.

"Elmer," I said, "what's going on? Why haven't we done like four more of these New Haven house flips by now?"

"Daniel, what do you mean 'we'? I've already done three more of these," he replied.

"Come again?" I said. "You've flipped three more properties down in New Haven, and you didn't call me?"

"I wanted to get something going on my own." Now I was furious.

"Are you fucking kidding me?" I shouted into the phone while trying to regain my composure. "Elmer, that's not how you do business. You don't short your partners. Relationships are way more important than a little bit of money; they're the holy grail in this business!" It was like I was reliving the fallout with Don all over again.

"Fuck you, Daniel," he replied, "I don't owe you anything!" I was beyond the point of being angry—I couldn't understand why he'd be so thoughtless. After I processed everything, I tried to calm down. The way Don and I had split hadn't just squandered a good business opportunity for both of us. It had also destroyed a friendship that we both cherished, and over what? Elmer and I were not nearly as close as Don and I had been, but I could already see some parallels and knew I didn't want to make the same mistakes twice.

Despite my anger, I forced myself to consider that maybe Elmer hadn't acted out of malice. I knew the guy, and he hadn't had the same benefits I'd had or the kind of mentors who taught him leadership and relationship skills. He was skeptical, mistrusting and afraid of big opportunities. Maybe it was a misunderstanding.

There was still plenty of use in us teaming up together, so I decided he might deserve a second chance. More importantly, the idealist in me felt that I could help right a wrong and perhaps prevent it from being perpetuated with me and elsewhere in the future.

"Elmer, I'm coming up to New Haven," I finally said at the end of the call. "Let's get together and talk about this."

When I arrived, I had Elmer drive us around town while he told me about all the deals I'd missed out on. I was pissed off, sure, but after talking to him, I could tell that Elmer was still thinking so small.

"Elmer, I can put this behind us, but you can't just ignore me," I said. "You don't cut people out like that. We did one together. I imagined we'd do at least the next several together. If you think you know everything I know or you've gotten all the value you can get from me, you're sorely mistaken." I tried to explain to him that it wasn't the money I was upset about. It was that we had rapport. We had a flag in the ground together—why not take it to the next level and build on that relationship?

As we were driving around the block of the four-family

we'd flipped, I saw a severely beaten two-building apartment complex on a large lot.

"Stop the car," I said. He saw I was looking at the property, and he quickly cut in.

"Daniel, you don't want nothing to do with that property, man," he said quickly. "They call it 'The Cage' around here. It's the shittiest property in New Haven."

"Just stop the car," I said. "I want to see what's going on over here."

He pulled over, and we both got out. Elmer wasn't wrong; the place was decrepit—there was graffiti, mold on the walls, caved-in ceilings, exposed wires everywhere and drug dealers lurking in the shadows. Even so, it had some of the same value propositions as 66 Chapel Street had: it was not even a mile from Yale, and it was a huge lot with a meaningful number of well-sized, rentable units.

I started walking up to the place like I owned it when a tenant came out smoking a long cigarette—a Marlboro 100. She took one look at me in my suit and asked if I was the new owner. I shook my head.

"My cable's out!" she said. "They cut my cable! Is someone going to fix this or what?"

"Sorry, ma'am, I'm not the new owner," I replied. "But if you give me the owner's number, maybe I can help you get your cable back." Sure enough, she went back inside and came back out with it. I had seen enough. Whoever oversaw the place had no idea what they were doing, and they were clearly neglecting it beyond belief. It was another drecky investment, which was my favorite kind. All I could see was potential.

After a few moments, I got back in the car with Elmer.

"Daniel, are you insane?" he said, eyes bugging out of his head. "The place is a crack house. There are drug dealers in and out of here day and night, prostitutes, anything you could think of! It's a complete shit hole!" He would have kept going, but I cut him off.

"Elmer, we're going to flip The Cage," I said calmly. "I'm going to give you a second chance here so we can do this the right way. Together."

Elmer had told me before that he didn't have much money, and more specifically, he didn't have money to come in on the deal. Even so, I knew he had been a solid property manager for the Maidmans, and he was good in the last deal. Plus, he was quick on his feet and on the ground in New Haven, which I couldn't be. I had to bring him in however I could because I knew it would work out for both of us.

"Listen, Elmer," I said, "if you're with me on this, you don't need to have the money up front. I'll lend you the money you need to come in on the deal, and I'll give you 10 percent of the investment, for which you will be responsible. For that, you'll put in the sweat equity towards making this a great deal. I just need you to be my eyes and ears on the ground as we do this." He couldn't believe what he was hearing, but even he could see what a good opportunity it was. After a little more conversation, he finally agreed to help me out.

After Rachel finished her last year of law school, our relationship was as serious as it had ever been. I saw how quickly things in my life were moving, and for all the ventures that were ahead, I knew I wanted Rachel by my side. The time had come to take the next step.

"Pack a bag," I told her one day after work. "We're going

to Atlantic City this weekend." She was excited at the news
—we had spent a romantic weekend there together months
before, and it had been the first time I told her I loved her.
But the truth was we weren't really going there again.

With her bag in hand, we headed towards the buses on
the lower point of Manhattan. As we approached, we turned
away from the bus station and towards a private helipad that
was nearby. Rachel's eyes widened.

"Where are we going?" she asked, an excited edge in her
voice. I smiled.

"You'll see," I said.

As we walked up, I confirmed my reservation with the
desk, and they took Rachel and me across the tarmac,
helping us into a helicopter. Even if I was making some
money at the time, a helicopter flight was well out of my
budget (as was the limo I'd rented that was going to pick us
up after we landed). Rather than paying out of pocket, I
arranged several barters with the helicopter tour business
and the limo business in exchange for their services: they
would get to advertise on my sign in Chelsea in exchange for
helping me set up my elaborate romantic gesture.

As the rotors whirred, the wind picked up, and soon we
were airborne above the water, looking down on the island of
Manhattan. The engagement ring I'd bought was burning a
hole in my pocket. My original intention was to have the
pilot fly us closer to the Hamptons, but there was something
so perfect about being above the city and looking down on
everything that I couldn't resist.

"Rachel," I said, pulling the ring out. "I love and cherish
the time we've spent together so far, but I want the rest of it

together too. Will you marry me?" She covered her face as tears filled her eyes.

"Yes!" she replied. From the cockpit, the pilot peeked over and gave a whoop that was hard to hear over the helicopter blades. When Rachel and I landed back in Manhattan, the limo I rented was waiting to pick us up at the heliport. We drove to a hotel I had rented in Sag Harbor for the weekend, where we celebrated, drank wine and watched the waves roll in. While we were in the Hamptons, we stopped by Rabbi Levi Baumgarten of Chabad for his blessing—and finally, we came back to the city to break the good news and celebrate with our friends.

9

FROM THE CAGE TO SHERMAN GARDENS

Back in New York, I was juggling a hefty workload for the senior partners at Hartman & Craven, all while trying to track down the mysterious owner of The Cage, who avoided my calls for several months. After finally getting him and playing phone tag for a couple more weeks, we finally set a time to speak and meet in person over the weekend in New Haven.

I drove up with Rachel in my 1973 Chevy Caprice Classic (which I affectionately called The Red Sled) the next weekend and readied myself for the negotiations that were sure to follow. I found the address and was surprised to see that I had pulled up in front of an opulent church with a fancy Mercedes parked out front, which was out of place in contrast to the relatively poor community surrounding it. All the same, I went in and announced myself.

"Is Lonnell here?" I called out.

"That's me," a voice replied from a side room. "Come in here and sit down."

Rachel and I followed his voice into a side room where we finally saw Lonnell, sitting at the head of the table and dressed in a nice fur. He was the local reverend! To his right was his "consultant," who was sitting quietly and sizing me up. It was clear that Lonnell was no typical pastor. I couldn't tell for sure, but it seemed like he was taking advantage of his tenants by neglecting his properties so badly and was perhaps not the ambassador of the cloth that he feigned to be. I tried to shake the uncertainty and confusion out of my mind because I had to focus up—it was game time.

"Hi, Lonnell," I replied, shaking his hand. "I recently visited one of your properties, and I have a proposition for you." With that, I took out a one-sheet option agreement I had drafted and started breaking it down in detail. I told Lonnell that it was clear The Cage was falling into disrepair and that it would be a hassle to pay to fix it up. In all, there were 22 units in two two-story buildings on an acre and a half of land, and my contract offered to buy the whole thing for $750,000. From the beginning, I could tell that Lonnell was in trouble, and my research confirmed he was in fore-closure.

"I have no interest in selling," Lonnell said. That didn't mean anything to me—my guess was nobody had offered him this much money up front before.

"I understand that," I said, "but maybe you'll let us convince you. It would be a great arrangement for both of us." After walking him through more of the details—and after Rachel had charmed him with flattering conversation—he started warming up to the idea.

"Well, I don't sign anything without my guy looking it over," Lonnell said, gesturing to the man sitting quietly to his right. Quite frankly, I don't think his guy knew what he was reading—but I said that was fine.

"Take your time," I responded. "My fiancée and I will be sitting outside." After waiting for a little while, we were called back in—and Lonnell said that we had a deal! We signed the contract on the spot, and I gave him $1,500 to make it binding. After shaking hands again, we assured Lonnell that he had made the right decision, and we were on our way back to New York.

I called Scott Hurwitz again to be my lawyer on the deal and explained that, like 66 Chapel Street, Elmer was going to help me on the ground. With that, we formed a limited liability company that would bear the new name of the property once it was finished: Sherman Gardens LLC. Now all I had to do was take a little time to gather up the rest of the money, and I'd be on my way. What I had not counted on was getting another call from the reverend two weeks later.

"Daniel, I'm sorry, but I don't think I'm going to sell you the property after all," he said. I had to hold in a laugh.

"What?" I replied. "What do you mean?"

"I don't think you're paying me enough," he said. He explained that he was in foreclosure and that the money we'd agreed on wouldn't be enough to bail him out and leave him some excess cash. "You have to pay me a million for it, or I'm not selling." I couldn't believe the balls he had, but there really wasn't anything to discuss.

"Reverend, respectfully," I said, "I don't appreciate you suggesting we don't have a deal. We shook hands in person, and you took money from me, but more importantly, you signed a contract. And just in case you're thinking of not selling it to me, I promise you—you may not sell it to me, but you're not going to sell it to anyone else either. I'll file a lien on your property." The call didn't end well, and the rest of it had to be talked through between our lawyers. Despite his objections, I was confident he would abide by the contract because he had no legal ground to stand on otherwise.

Shortly thereafter, I secured some short-term leverage I would use to buy the property. I didn't have the money to renovate yet, but I was working on financing the deal and orchestrating the execution of all the next steps—sourcing, structuring, managing, marketing and so on. With another 10 percent kicked in from David Zarabi, we were on our way.

"I'm glad you're getting this done," David said. "This is a perfect launch pad for you." Like Kurt and me, David always related to the underdog mentality—and he was so confident in my abilities, he didn't even feel the need to see the property before putting up money.

About two weeks before closing, the local NBC station ran a story on The Cage—and on all the blight and chaos it was causing in the neighborhood. In the middle of it, they echoed what Elmer had said to me before: that it was "the worst property in New Haven." Once again, Elmer called me in a panic.

"This is it, Daniel!" Elmer yelled over the phone. "We're fucked!"

"Elmer, calm down," I said. "What they just did on the news is the best thing that could've happened to us. That kind of publicity is going to be worth a million dollars on the back end! Just keep doing what you're doing; it's going to be fine."

With only a few days left before closing, Elmer disappeared. I needed him at the property, and he was nowhere to be found. After calling and calling for a few days, I finally got a hold of him. Once again, he was panicking.

"This is too much pressure, Daniel," he said, hyperventilating. "I can't do this deal. I can't do it!" Once again, I talked him up and convinced him that everything wasn't going to fall apart.

"Just stay calm and let's see this through," I said. "I'm headed to the property now, and I need you to meet me there." When we finally arrived, there was another surprise waiting for us: the reverend had come by to steal back all the appliances from the empty apartments. All the microwaves, stoves and refrigerators were gone. Elmer couldn't believe it and was on the verge of another panic attack, but to me, it was a blessing in disguise.

"I think he did us a favor!" I said, clapping a hand on Elmer's shoulder to calm him down. "I don't want the scrap metal. Let's put new stuff in." I didn't know where I would get the money to do it, but I knew I would figure it out.

Shortly after closing, I invited my dad down to look at my newest investment. As soon as he got out of his car, I excitedly explained the intricacies of the deal, my plans for the property and what I thought the potential upside was. As he looked around and took in the broken windows and debris everywhere, he was dumbfounded.

"Daniel, you're fucking crazy," he said to me—my father rarely if ever swore, so his words packed a punch. "This place is a shit show! You're going to get killed over here!" I frowned. It was frustrating not to have his immediate support, but it was too late anyway.

"Dad, it's already done," I said. "But don't worry—this is

going to be great!" Unfortunately, the next problem was already on its way.

"Daniel," Scott told me over the phone, "I've got bad news. The city wants to condemn the property." On the surface this might've made sense because it was so rundown. I saw the truth of what was happening: the city was run by aldermen who wanted to take over the property however they could. Sure enough, their justification was that they needed the land to build senior living housing. Seeing the headache ahead, I thought maybe it was time to just get out right there and then.

"Maybe we can just flip it back to the city?" I suggested to Scott. It seemed like a way to make at least a little profit and avoid hassle on a deal gone bad, but the city didn't want to pay up—they clearly had their own plans for the neighborhood. It looked like if my investment was going to pay off, I would have to do everything I could to stop the condemnation proceedings. It would be an uphill battle every step of the way. After doing some reading, I called Elmer, who was already busy drumming up potential subcontractors around town who could work on the renovations when the time was right.

"Elmer," I said, "I've done the legal research. The city wants to condemn, but they can't take it by eminent domain, so they will want to argue it's abandoned or neglected. To prevent that, we need to pull permits—any permits. I don't care what they're for, Elmer. I just need you to pull as many permits as you can, whether it's for general repairs, window replacements or whatever."

"We're going to lose everything on this, aren't we?"

Elmer said, clearly panicking. "We're so screwed. We're going to get killed here!"

"Calm down," I said. "If we pull permits, we're fixing and repairing a property—and if we're fixing a property, they can't say it's neglected or condemnable. Just pull the permits. We're going to be fine."

I knew that turning The Cage into Sherman Gardens would be a lot of work, but it seemed like every second, there was a new problem leaping out from around the corner with a bat to shake us down. While fighting off condemnation proceedings, the next issue was an active and organized crack-dealing operation on the grounds that was scaring people away—and unlike some of the behind-the-scenes legal headaches, I knew this was something I'd have to deal with myself.

Once again, I drove to New Haven in modest but professional clothes. After seeing one guy out front who clearly was doing drug deals, I walked up confidently to announce myself.

"Hey man, listen," I said politely. "You're doing whatever you have to do here, and it's none of my business. But cleaning up this property is my job." I was careful not to reveal that I owned the property. "I need to do my job, or I'll have problems on my end, and I know you can respect that point," I said. "I work for the management of the ownership of this property, and it's my responsibility to renovate and clear stuff out here. There's going to be a lot of activity here, and it's not going to be quiet like it was. No disrespect here. I'm just doing my job. But I wanted to let you know."

It was a speech I would have to give a handful of times to many different drug dealers, but fortunately, I never had any altercations. Even so, they weren't totally sure I meant business and that there actually would be any activity, so they still weren't clearing out. That was fine, I figured; I would just create the activity myself.

The next step was to hire laborers and subcontractors to start working on the units. Their job at first was to board up windows and doors and to reboard them if any dealers tried to take the boards down. We also hired a contractor who happened to have a cousin in the New Haven Police Department—and fortunately, the officer took it upon himself to check up on his cousin daily! Right away, I saw an opportunity.

"Elmer, make sure those police officers stay around the site," I said. "I want people running them coffee and doughnuts every time they're there, talking to them as much as they can. Create a little substation for them." Sure enough, as the police started coming around more and more, the drug dealers started clearing out and moving down the street. As we kept cleaning out units, it turned out that there were some appliances left behind after all—we found some digital scales for weighing crack in some of the empty apartments that must've been worth $2,000 each.

In the process of getting everything ready for a full-gut renovation, most of the people who were living there were non-paying tenants who had to leave the property. While I was overseeing that one day, I saw one of the tenants who had come to clear out some of his stuff had pulled up in a limo.

"Hey, what's going on?" I asked him. "You haven't paid rent in like six months—what's with the limo?" He flashed me back the biggest smile.

"I won the New Haven lottery," he said. "I'm out of here!"

With everyone cleared out, we gutted the place like a hog and upgraded electric, put up new drywall and replaced fixtures. We put in new appliances, redid the bathrooms, put up new siding, fixed the ceilings and added a host of other improvements. Finally, 12 months later, it was finished, and we were ready to fill it with tenants.

Before we had renovated, the old landlord had his tenants paying as much as $1,000 per unit to live in a dangerous place that wasn't cared for. After everything we'd done to it, we had a brand new, renovated building with four-bedroom apartments in it that went for as much as $1,500 each—and thanks to the hustling he'd done while I was in New York, Elmer already had plenty of new tenants lined up. The place was so nice that one of the old tenants even moved back in, and she couldn't have been happier with the changes.

Though the project was close to the finish line, I knew we needed one last PR push to fill the rest of the rent roll. I remembered the negative local NBC spot from before, so I looked up the reporter, Brandon Rudat, and started cold calling him. After hunting him down incessantly, I finally got him on the phone.

"Hey, Brandon," I said. "I remembered your spot on The Cage from about 18 months ago, but it's a totally new place now. We're calling it Sherman Gardens, and it's absolutely beautiful. You guys have done so many negative stories on the old version of the property, but this is an uplifting story that you have to see for yourself. Your viewers will love it!" I didn't even know the guy, but that didn't stop me from pitching him a PR story!

"I'll tell you what," he said to me. "I can be there tomorrow at 6:30 am. If you can be there, we can quickly shoot it." With that, I told him it was a done deal, and I took the early train into New Haven. Sure enough, the news vans pulled up the next day, and I made my television debut. Soon after that story, everybody wanted to move in.

It wasn't entirely clear how Sherman Gardens would make money for everyone from the beginning—would we hold it as an asset or just sell it off? Eventually, it was becoming clear that the return on our time sweat equity wasn't particularly high. All the driving back and forth from New York City to New Haven all the time was starting to add up. When it comes to running an asset like a big apartment building, I found that it was like making soup—you couldn't turn your back on it, and you had to keep stirring, which was difficult to do at a distance. Eventually, it seemed like the best idea would be to sell it, build a reputation and "put one on the board," so to speak. Finally, we listed the deal.

Not long after, I got a call from a broker who had an investor interested in buying Sherman Gardens. The woman's name was Ruth, and she was from New Jersey. I hadn't even met her or the broker who introduced her, but even so, I was ready to sell. I sent Elmer to meet with Ruth and the broker a few times, and everything seemed like it was going smoothly. They negotiated a contract, and Ruth escrowed a $125,000 deposit, which was great—but then, things got complicated. Right before we were set to close, Ruth went into default with no financing, and it looked like

it was all going to fall through. I had to consult with my partners on the project to see what the next move was.

"You should keep the deposit and refinance," David said.
It made sense—the $125,000 was free money at that point,
and refinancing would enable us to satisfy our existing debt
obligations, take out tax-free proceeds and retain a stabilized,
income-producing asset. Even so, I didn't want to do it.

"I don't want to keep it," I said to him. "I don't want to
just take this woman's money. I'd rather give her more time.
Maybe she'll find the financing, and I'll just have her add to
the deposit and provide us some healthy releases, so we don't
have to worry about her playing any games pre- or post-
closing."

After talking it through, that was the plan—but I wanted
some additional security. In addition to collecting another
$125,000, I had her sign a release saying she would never
suggest in the future that something was amiss or wrong with
any terms of our deal or that any representations were made,
but rather that she was doing her own diligence and not
relying on us (in case there was to be future litigation).

She signed the amendment to the contract, and we were
back to waiting. As irony would have it, she repeated her
blunder a second time, and again, I allowed her to add
money to the deposit and sign yet another release—you
cannot make this shit up.

Finally, with a little more time added on, she scraped the
funds together and was able to close on the property in
December 2005 for the highest per-unit price in New Haven
history—and I was happier than a pig in shit. The total cost
basis for me, David and Elmer—including the $750,000 we
initially paid for the property, all the new appliances, labor,

closing costs and what have you—was about $1.3 million. Now, we were turning around and selling it for $2.5 million! Elmer and David made roughly $100,000 each for their respective 10 percent. I owned the other 80 percent of the deal, and it was structured that way because it was so risky; I didn't want to expose my friends and partners to unnecessary risk if everything blew up (and wanted to keep as much upside as possible, of course).

Fortunately, it had paid off huge—it was the first time I had made nearly one million dollars off *one property!* Having that money in my account was life-changing, but it wasn't the cash that mattered. It was the fact that I'd done it my way. I had mended a relationship with Elmer and hopefully taught him something about friendship. I'd brought my friend David into the deal. And I'd closed a truly big deal—all from the worst property imaginable. The momentum and the energy were tremendous, and all I could think about was what I would do next.

10

BUILDING MOMENTUM

In November 2004, Rachel and I were married in Miami Beach at the Royal Palm. It was an intimate wedding with only 96 guests, though it included people who flew in from Israel to California and back to be there.

The ceremony was beautiful and complete with all the traditional Jewish traditions. My sister Alisa gave a moving speech, and a friend of the family sang a song in Hebrew that had everyone in attendance teary-eyed. The weekend began with a Shabbat barbecue on Friday night, followed by a night of celebrating and dancing. On Saturday, we were wed, and on Sunday, we had brunch and took over the lobby of the hotel—again dancing and celebrating while the other hotel guests looked on.

The years had passed quickly since I'd started practicing law, and for the longest time, I kept feeling like I hadn't lit my fire yet. With Sherman Gardens finally behind me, the fire was finally lit. Hartman & Craven was still my day job, but behind the scenes, I was looking for deals in New York City as often as I could. Renovating and owning real estate in New York City had always been my dream, and having a hand in making New York City what it was signified "making it" for me more than anything else. It was what "being on the map" meant, in my mind.

Though my father had been skeptical of Sherman Gardens at first, he'd seen how well I'd done and was impressed with what I'd accomplished. With my appetite for deals larger than ever and my father's increased confidence in my abilities, I decided the next venture I did would be with him. Really, it would be *for* him.

"Dad, we have to get out of single-family rentals and into something bigger," I told him on the phone one day. "There's a great place I've been looking at in the Bronx near Little Italy. It's a beautiful turn-of-the-century building right on the edge of Arthur Avenue, near Mike's Deli."

"That's a great area," my father said. "What are the details?"

"It's two stories, 29 units and two stores," I replied. "They're asking 2.8 million."

"Daniel, where will I raise all that money for one investment?" I wasn't surprised to hear him ask that. My father was an astute investor but conservative when it came to investing. He never wanted to stretch beyond his means. But I already had a plan in mind—I just knew I would have to talk him into it.

"This is just like Leratex, the textile factory your parents started at 110 Eldridge Street on the Lower East Side after World War II," I said. "We're going to sell one of your investment properties, the single-family at 21 Hicks Lane in Great

Neck, to make this work. Then, we'll get financing." Though I could tell I'd moved him a little, he was still uncertain.

"Let me handle the details of the deal," I said. "I promise you the upside here is enormous. What do you say?" After realizing what a great long-term investment it would be for my sister and me (as well as any grandchildren we might have), he was in—and in honor of keeping the investment so legacy-minded, we named the building's entity name Leratex in honor of my grandparents.

As I mentioned before, my dad had bought our family's "chicken coop" rental house in approximately 1983 for only $38,000, and he'd been renting it to a carpenter named Jay Fili, who remains a dear friend of the family to this day. Jay wanted to buy the house outright because it was set up perfectly for him to store his tools, but my dad didn't want to give up the house and be out a piece of income-earning property. Instead, he decided to do a 1031 exchange with the tenant carpenter.

Named after the tax code, a 1031 exchange allows an investor to sell their investment property while simultaneously (or within 180 days) buying another property or asset of like value, thus deferring capital gains taxes. Put even more simply, it's a tax-advantaged way to swap one investment property for a similar one and is effectively a modern-day barter.

When my father went to sell the chicken coop, he tasked Jay with finding another house on Long Island, buying it and then trading it with him for the house he actually wanted. After some extensive scouting and paperwork, Jay found and contracted a house on 28 Hicks Lane. In 1992, my dad and Jay completed the trade. My dad had collected a healthy rent on 28 Hicks Lane in the many years since—and now, we were going to sell it.

Property in Great Neck had greatly appreciated since 1992, so my dad's initial investment of $38,000 was now worth considerably more. After listing the house with a friend, we were able to sell it for $718,000—but we still weren't done. With that part of the deal closed, I took the details of our Bronx deal to a friend, Elliott Birnbaum of Meridian Capital. Eliott had become a good friend while I worked at Maidman & Mittelman because he repped some of my clients as their broker. I knew he did great work and was an honorable guy, and I knew he would be the perfect person to do business with on the deal my father and I were working on. With his agreement, we brought in Eliott to broker the debt to a regional bank and combine it with my father's cash proceeds.

Through Eliott's expertise, New York Community Bank issued a term sheet for a loan for the approximate amount of $1.8 million, to be combined with approximately $700,000 of equity from the sale of 28 Hicks Lane. With the structure and funding in place, I closed on the building on my father's behalf. Our arrangement was that I would be his operating partner, and in the long term, it would inure to the benefit of my sister and me (and perhaps to children of our own one day). From my dad's initial $38,000 investment in the 1980s, we had leveraged our way into a property that was worth $2.5 million (and has since appreciated to approximately $6 million today).

Though the bones of the building were good, there was a lot of renovation to do and plenty of problems to fix. Before long, I was spending most of my free time there—one day I'd be in the basement looking at boiler problems, and the next I'd be trying to find creative ways to resolve building violations. We closed the deal in December 2005, but the real work was only beginning. Just like Sherman Gardens, running a bigger, multi-purpose building required time, attention and resources. There were apartments to keep leased, repairs and maintenance to do, tech upgrade efficiencies to add, collections and a host of other management items to handle—meanwhile I was a shop of one person, and I also happened to have a serious day job. My father helped, and we had some fun running around up there together, but I wanted to absorb the brunt of it.

Although getting Leratex up to speed and filled with tenants while juggling a full-time law job would be more than enough for most people, my appetite for bigger and bigger real estate deals was becoming insatiable. The PR story I'd persuaded the local NBC news station to pick up was getting a lot of traction (and I was showing it to any and every investor I took a meeting with to build my reputation). Meanwhile, my friends from Great Neck were growing in their own careers, and many of them had money saved to invest. Nearly everyone in my circle had talked about investing or going into business together, but the timing had never been right. Still, with Sherman Gardens behind me, those airy and aspirational conversations were about to materialize in a major way. After seeing what I'd done in Connecticut, my friends were ready to jump in with me.

"Daniel, we've been talking about this forever," Ari said to me one day. "We need to start buying buildings. Let's find a property that makes sense." It was exactly what I wanted to hear. And so when I wasn't at the office, I was hunting for deals. Eventually, I found an 1890s tenement building in the South Bronx that I fell in love with almost immediately. Aside from having aged charm, it also had a massive 30 by 70-foot illuminated sign on the roof facing the Bruckner Expressway. The sign was visible from all directions, but particularly from the Triborough Bridge. There was plenty of value in the building itself, but I knew my billboard expertise would be an add-on that could give us an edge.

The property was an industrial, desolate block off the Bruckner Expressway that I wanted to call industrial chic, though it wasn't chic yet. It was in Mott Haven, which was beset by crime and gang activity at the time (though it has since been developed and is now known as SoBro). In all, it was a 20-unit, $3.3 million property.

Knowing the city's history, I could imagine the story of why such a beautiful building fell into disrepair: after World War II, there was a huge increase in public works projects, and the result was that a lot of industry built up around the Bronx. The Bruckner Expressway to the south had cut off the entire neighborhood from the rest of the communities around it. The relative social isolation and industrial activity had no doubt driven property values down, and things had gradually gone to seed. Even so, I didn't see a neglected area —I saw a historic building that would give working professionals an affordable place to live, one stop on the No.6 train from Manhattan.

I brought the opportunity to Ari, and he was interested, so the next step was to find out more about the current ownership. As I discovered, the owners were a trio of seedy guys. As we were touring the building, one of the three partners began explaining how he dealt with evicting particularly difficult tenants.

"It's funny, really," he said. "The way I get those tough units empty is I go in with 25 rats in a cage, shake it up a bit and let them loose. It drives the tenants crazy!" Privately, I was horrified—what they were doing was completely illegal! Even so, I kept my mouth shut. The three guys clearly had a dysfunctional partnership and were showing their discord in front of us. It was in poor form, and it was also more than reflected in the property. They were openly fighting over what to do with their asset going forward—some of them allegedly wanted to keep it while others wanted to sell and move on.

Meanwhile, their investment was languishing. Any so-called renovations they'd done consisted of patching together holes in the walls and other shoddy work that hadn't resulted in anything functional. In other words, it was the perfect opportunity for Ari and me to jump in and take it off their hands.

Ari and I only had three weeks to close the deal, so we got to work right away. To put things in motion, we would have to sign a hard contract confirming a $150,000 deposit with no possibility of a refund. It meant that we needed to complete all our diligence before signing the contract, then raise the money and get financing quickly or else all our money would be forfeited.

It was a serious risk. Although Ari had some money at the time from his own business ventures like I did, neither of us had that kind of cash to waste. We also gained the impression that other buyers were looking to tie up the deal. Even so, the upside was undeniable—and I knew we had an advantage. The only reason I signed was because of an old friend named Gideon. Gideon worked for RCG Longview, the lender we were approaching. From third grade, I'd known Gideon to be a strait-laced and studious person. We were friends then and acquaintances throughout the years, but what I knew above all was that Gideon wasn't a bullshitter and that he would follow through on his word. After Ari and I had done the legwork of running the title, clearing the environmental issues and providing the financials, Gideon assured us he could deliver the loan. Based on my knowledge of his character, I knew the deal wouldn't fall through if we wanted it.

From the beginning, Ari and I spent nearly all our time together working every angle imaginable. There were value engineering problems to solve, investors to seek out and a growing number of people to keep informed and on the same page. On the first leg, we had to lock up the deal and agree on a business path. After that, we had to raise the money and secure the bank debt. As a testament to the painstaking thought that went into every aspect of the deal, we even went back and forth for hours coming up with the name for our LLC.

Eventually, Ari and I settled on First Bronx LLC as a holding company and put pen to paper in early 2005. It was more risk than we should've taken on at that juncture, but we leaped with faith and on the strength of our friendship. First Bronx was automatically a milestone for Ari and me since it was our first building together, and we had to do it right. After we had gotten $2.3 million from RCG Longview, we set about raising another $1.3 million from friends and family members.

To syndicate the deal, we called everyone we knew who had an appetite for real estate investing. On a usual syndication, you would charge the investors certain fixed fees for entering the investment. Because we were cutting our teeth, sourcing from our network on a high-risk project and short on time, we only charged a management fee and no promote —we just needed to raise the equity and fast. Many of our closest friends put significant money in the deal—and Kurt even joined in as well.

At the time, Kurt didn't have a tremendous amount of money to spend; even so, he and his wife concluded they wanted to expand their investment horizons, and they put up $25,000. After receiving the check, I knew I had to call to thank him.

"Kurt, we appreciate this so much," I told him on the phone. "We're going to make everything back and then some on this one." Maybe I wanted to assure him he'd made the right decision, but he brushed my concerns aside.

"We're investing in *you*, Danny," he said. The check he and Marcie wrote wasn't the biggest figure we saw throughout the funding process, but it was the one that meant the most to me. It was the ultimate vote of confidence —and it gave me the strength I needed not to fail.

Though I had profits I'd made from Sherman Gardens, the money was tied up in other investments and costs, and I wasn't entirely liquid. To make sure I had equal equity in the deal as Ari, Ari's father offered to front me the money so that Ari and I could be equal partners. With that settled, we were on our way.

Throughout the deal, Ari and I both handled investors and the business end of things while I was on the ground in charge of the renovations. Shortly into the renovation, I realized the magnitude of what I had taken on. The building was 18,000 square feet, and while it had beautiful bones, it was in shambles. I had *never* done construction management of this magnitude before, and even with all my creativity and value-engineering ideas, there was no way we had enough money on our own to pull it off. I had to break the news to Ari, but in classic Ari fashion, he couldn't have been calmer about it.

"Let's figure out how to get it done," he said. "If we have to make a capital call, so be it." It meant that Ari and I had to put in additional equity and that we had to call everyone we'd already asked and ask for more as well. I hadn't felt anxious about making the initial ask, but the second phone call made me feel uneasy. Even so, it had to be done, and nobody had lost confidence in our ability to get the project done.

On one of the first days checking things out, Ari came by to meet with the contractors and me. Sure enough, I pulled up and parked in an SUV. A little while later, Ari pulled up in a purple Porsche, and my eyes nearly bugged out of my head.

"Ari, what are you doing?" I said. "You can't do that here!"

"What do you mean?" he asked, half-laughing and calm as ever as he stepped out and shut the driver's side door. "I'm on time, aren't I?"

"Not that," I said. "Your car. You can't drive here in that!"

He paused and squinted his eyes at me like I was speaking another language. Fortunately, the contractors weren't on-site yet, so I had a minute to explain. "First, you can't bring a Porsche like that to this neighborhood—you've got to park around the corner, or you're liable to get your wheels stolen. Second, if the contractors see that car, they're going to charge us more! We're supposed to be a couple of two-bit real estate investors, remember?"

"Well, maybe *you* are, Daniel," Ari said with his signature Hollywood smile. Even so, he understood my point—and after that first meeting, I often dealt with the contractors on the front-end while Ari and I conferred behind the scenes on all major decisions.

From the beginning, First Bronx was a welcome challenge. We would have to get incredibly creative and strip the project down to its absolute essence. But around every corner was a new problem. The first step was to clear the building of remnant tenants, and right away, there was one guy who refused to leave.

"We can't renovate with him in there," one of the lead contractors told me. "We may have to pack up until you're ready for us."

"Don't go anywhere," I told him firmly. "I'll deal with this." I marched into the building to find the stubborn tenant. His name was Juan, and he was an unassuming guy from Mexico. He seemed like a nice enough guy, as it turned out—despite the fact that he wouldn't leave and we needed him to. He wasn't trying to give us a hard time; he was just out of work and didn't have anywhere else to go. I figured if I couldn't convince him to get out, maybe I could turn his unwillingness to leave into an asset that would allow my project to go forward.

"Hey, Juan," I said to him. "I understand you can't leave,

but I need to keep construction on pace here. What would you say if I let you stay in the building and paid you to be my security? You could make sure the site stays safe and everything is in order. How does that sound?" Because it was a rough area, it wasn't unusual for petty thieves to break into buildings and steal copper piping or wiring. Having someone on-site at all times could help us avoid a similar outcome.

After talking it through, it sounded good to him—and we pushed forward. We got to know each other a little better over the next few months, and he told me that he planned to move out of New York and buy land in Mexico. Once I heard that, I knew what to do. Rather than battle back and forth, I cut him a check for $12,000 to go buy his first tract of land in Mexico, and he was over the moon. It might've been an expensive buyout, but it was a small cost to pay to create a win-win and get the building cleared.

With him gone, it was time to do some serious value engineering—stretching our dollars and finding or creating value in the property in ways that were easy to overlook. One of the first items on my to-do list was to get a quote from an architect to draw up plans for the place. He came back and told me it would cost $30,000. Though the expense was one thing, the bigger factor was that the more time that passed, the longer it would take to see our renovations through and the more interest we would have to pay on our loan. We couldn't afford to waste much time, but I didn't know what else to do.

Exploring the grounds that day, I came across an old, locked gang box the prior owners must've left there. I didn't have the lock combination, but I got some help prying it open. Sure enough, inside were a complete set of fully drawn architectural plans. The work I was about to pay through the nose for was already done! I pulled the architect's phone number off the plans and gave him a call.

"Hey, listen," I said, "I'm over at 700 East 134th Street. I'm the new owner of the property. I was about to hire someone to draft plans for the place, but from what I'm holding in my hands here, it looks like you've already done that. What's the story here?"

"The story is I did a ton of work for the previous owners, and I'm still owed $6,000," the architect replied. "We had a deal in place, and they flaked on our arrangement." I thought for a moment before replying.

"What if I were to pay your remaining balance?" I asked. "All I need in return is to get these plans refined and approved as quickly as possible." It was enough to get the architect into action, and I had already saved First Bronx LLC thousands of dollars—but more importantly, it gave us time to draw up plans and then get them approved by the Department of Buildings.

Once the plans were in place, I met with another round of vendors. The next problem was the staircases.

"These things are no good," one of the consultants said. "You're going to have to rip them out entirely and put in new ones." Again, the cost they were suggesting was completely prohibitive—and it also made no sense. The staircases were turn-of-the-century steel with hand-crafted bluestone steps, wooden handrails and iron guardrails. They obviously had a history dating all the way back to the very initial construction of the building! They might have been tarnished and damaged, but it was impossible to look at them and not get romantic.

"Look, I understand these are busted up," I said, "but do we have to rip them out? You guys are the experts here, but could you take a closer look? Can't we shore them up and restore them? It would be a shame to let such a beautiful feature go to waste."

After reconsidering, the consultant said that actually, the staircases *were* structurally sound and, with a little work, we could replace the steps and handrails. After a little back and forth, we agreed to a price point, and once again, I had maintained the building's integrity and saved tens of thousands of dollars.

I was starting to see how this process would go. We would hire contractors and inspectors to come in, and their first instinct would be to catastrophize about things. Even so, they were highly credentialed people with their own egos and their own staff to take care of—of course, they would try to bid their projects higher (even if they weren't entirely conscious that they were doing it). My solution would be to go slowly, be respectful and second-guess every major spending decision. I was learning again and again that within every "no" way more wiggle room than there seemed to be—and that no one would steward Ari and my money as astutely as we would.

Day after day, I was peeling back layers of the tenement building and finding art and raw beauty. The next problem was that the plaster covering the walls in the hallways and apartments was crumbling.

"None of this plaster is any good anymore," the contractor said. "You're going to need to replace it all with drywall." Since I was on the scene that day, I took a hammer and smashed a bit of the wall out myself to see what was going on. Underneath the sheetrock was gorgeous, undamaged brick that had been smoked black—the old owners must've had a fire decades earlier. Immediately, I saw it as a blessing. The prevailing wisdom at the time was that the brick in old buildings shouldn't be exposed on the inside. Even so, I didn't care—I wasn't just going to expose it in the hallways, I was going to expose at least one wall in every apartment as well!

"Guys, hold on a minute," I said. "Forget sheetrock—why would I want to cover this? Brick is hip! It's retro, and all the tenants coming in here are young professionals from the city. They're going to love this. Let's get ten guys in here to rip all the plaster down." Sure enough, the brick was fine. From there, we exposed it, cleaned it with muriatic acid and sealed it, and I'd saved us another 15 grand or so at least.

Next on the list was that the building needed all new gas lines, which were quoted at $64,000 to fix. Again, that price tag was outrageous, and I knew there had to be another way. After thinking about it, I wondered: did the building even *need* gas lines? Why couldn't it all be electric? The gas lines were attached to gas ovens in the apartments, but the people we were targeting on the rental side weren't a bunch of home chefs. They didn't cook much; most of them probably ordered out. These were young professionals, entrepreneurs and artists.

As local real estate law clearly stated, stoves in their apartments were mandatory—but they didn't need gas stoves. What if we put electric stoves in all the units and gave the tenants one monthly bill instead of two for gas and electric? After doing the math, it made sense. We capped the main gas line and put in 220 electrical lines and stoves. The result was yet *another* savings of about $50,000. I imagined myself as a scrapper with limited resources but a specific end in mind. I was chipping away at a block of marble, but what was inside wasn't a beautiful statue; it was a perfectly constructed real estate deal—and the dust and stone chips left on the studio floor were all the expenses we couldn't afford.

At the same time, I was dealing with the super, a former semi-professional boxer with a lisp and a hearing aid who was a sweet man but who had a hell of a short fuse. He took me down to the boiler room and introduced me to yet another problem.

"This entire boiler is no good," he said. "It's going to need to be replaced." Replacing it would've cost $35,000, which did not work for me. Instead, I brought in boiler company after boiler company to see who could fix it as it was. After going through about four or five, one mechanic promised he could restore our ancient boiler—and instead of costing us $35,000, it was going to cost us just $6,500. As the super and I were about to head upstairs again with another problem solved, I saw a door in the corner of the basement that was previously obscured by drywall, garbage and boxes.

"What is that?" I asked him.

He shrugged. "Must be storage or something."

I got closer to investigate and moved some of the debris out of the way. I opened the door, and inside was a huge room that was clearly built to be an apartment—it was just filled with old boxes and ancient stacks of newspaper. My eyes lit up—could this really be an additional, rentable apartment nobody had mentioned until now? After looking at the original I-cards for the building, an old form of property record in New York City where the building details were on glorified index cards, it turned out that was exactly what it was—it just needed to be cleared out and cleaned up. After doing further diligence, we added it to the list of ongoing renovations. Just like that, our 20-unit building had become a 21-unit building!

No matter how many challenges the project was throwing at us, Ari and I kept tapping into our creativity and coming up with cost-saving solutions. The place was looking more and more beautiful every day, and it felt like we couldn't lose.

In between the wheeling and dealing Ari and I were doing in the Bronx, I was still working at Hartman & Craven every day and juggling 35 to 40 different client files. One day in December 2006, I got a letter addressed to my office at Hartman & Craven. It was almost a year to the day of closing the Sherman Gardens sale to Ruth—and here I was getting a letter from her and her attorney. I opened it up and read carefully. The letter alleged that I had fraudulently induced Ruth into buying Sherman Gardens and that I had misrepresented the deal; because of that, she was prepared to give me back the deed to the property in exchange for a full refund. The letter was so over-the-top that I had to laugh. After that, I called Scott, who had represented me in the deal.

"This is ridiculous," I told him over the phone. "It's a $2.5 million property with dozens of people involved and multiple amendments. I even had her sign additional paper-work waiving the right to claim any of the things she's claiming here—this isn't a fucking Verizon contract!"

"I totally agree with you," Scott said, "but it's not going

to stop her from trying to take you to court over this. I don't think you should budge because you have every proper release and piece of paperwork you need, but it's going to take time. You're looking at a potential multi-year litigation with insurance companies."

All I could do was put my head in my hands and let my lawyers do what they did best. I had never even met this woman or had any real interaction with her other than through lawyers, but she was becoming a problem that just wouldn't go away. The reality was that she was a sore loser. She was running her asset in absentia, and the results were weak collections. She was looking for an out even though she had no legal leg to stand on—but she was going to try her best to go back on the deal she'd made with me anyway.

I already knew what had happened to her because I sensed the danger of it happening to me on First Bronx. In a questionable neighborhood on a beat-up piece of property, you need to have hands-on management—and I knew she didn't have it. Ruth didn't even live in Connecticut, where Sherman Gardens was situated. She had absentee management who ran the property into the ground, and now she was looking for someone to blame. After a few more phone calls, I found out she was suing *everyone*—the broker, Elmer and our entity Sherman Gardens LLC. We would just have to spend the necessary time and money to prove we had no obligations to give her a refund.

Meanwhile, my father and I were still pouring time and money into Leratex—and he was starting to get antsy.

"Why aren't we making money yet?" he would call and ask me. I wasn't panicked—I knew how these deals worked, and I knew that on an investment like Leratex, the time horizon was a little bit longer, and it would take more time to take any money out—close to two or three years, in fact. We would be slower to get to the return, but for the time being, everything was going as well as it could be (run-of-the-mill renovation inconveniences aside).

"Dad, we're good," I replied calmly. "You've just got to be patient. We have to spend time growing and nurturing the rents on this place. We're going to make all our money back and then some." He already knew all that, of course, but I was an easy target—and I think the cynic in him enjoyed watching me sweat. I had always had very high standards for the deals I put together, and I also had a huge tolerance for stress and complexity. Even so, I had forgotten to consider one simple thing: when you and your dad work together on a business venture, he is always your toughest critic.

I was also realizing the management company we'd hired wasn't holding up their end of filling out the building. It was yet another reminder that nobody could run our money like I could myself, so I decided it was another thing I'd have to take into my own hands. My father and I agreed, and we fired the company, which meant I would have to be even more involved than I already was.

With so many things on my plate, every day had me getting up early to take personal phone calls, arriving at the office more than a little harried and scouting out my properties at night. Eventually, it was time for my annual performance review at Hartman & Craven—and I was bracing myself for the worst. I did good work, and the partners liked me—so much so that they gave me their most sensitive cases, knowing my ability to finesse even the most difficult clients. Even so, I clearly had a lot going on. When my time came, I sat down in a room surrounded by three or four of the senior partners. A lot of the feedback was good, and some of it was constructive, but one litigator had the final review, and I remember his words the most.

"You know, Daniel, you're a really good attorney," he said. "All the partners like you so much that they give you their own personal work on top of the in-house work. And your clients like you as well. But I have to be honest: you're all over the fucking place."

I bit the inside of my cheek to keep my face steady, but on the inside, I was trying not to laugh. I was in the middle of two different gut renovations, answering to 10 or 12 different law partners with 35 to 40 open case files, juggling the partners' families' legal affairs and the firm's all while managing my own properties, printing my own invoices, managing contractors, managing my father's investment expectations and putting out countless other daily fires. On top of it all, I was now also gearing up for a lawsuit that could drag on for years. They only knew a fraction of how all over the place I really was. All things considered, I thought I was doing pretty well!

11

WALKING THE TIGHTROPE

By 2007, I was about a year into both Leratex and First Bronx, and Leratex hadn't turned out to attract the local students from Fordham University my father and I thought it would. Instead, it was gradually becoming a working man's building that was almost entirely occupied, with the storefronts filling up as well. The renovation on First Bronx was almost finished as well, and we were filling it with tenants at a good clip. The surrounding area was still up-and-coming, but the building was barely recognizable compared to how it used to look. Instead of crumbling plaster and dirty walls, we had clean stairwells with their grand history restored and plenty of bright red brick everywhere.

On First Bronx, it was time to start aggressively pursuing potential tenants for the building that was largely my responsibility. For some additional help, Ari and I hired a local leasing agent named Sidney Miller, who had some experience filling out properties in the neighborhood. He was an older dude who had a trippy, hippie-ish vibe about him who was constantly stressing the need to fill the apartment with "hip" tenants. Even if it was questionable whether he even knew what that meant, he still had great energy that I knew would help sell apartments.

After work every day, Sid and I went to local bars in the Bronx and handed out fliers and pamphlets to advertise that we were renting out our building. Though there was some interest, we hadn't closed anyone yet, and I knew that psychologically, getting that first tenant in the building would make all the difference. One day, a woman walked up to me and introduced herself as Anaida Hernandez. She was a painter who had done some shows in the city and was looking for a new place to live.

"This apartment would be perfect for you," I said excitedly. "Come on, it's close enough that I can show you right now." After finishing our drinks, we walked over, and I showed her how beautiful the building was, along with touring one of the best units in the building.

"So, what do you think?" I asked her. She seemed uncertain.

"It's beautiful, Daniel," she said, "but there's no way I can afford to live here." I tried to talk her into it for a minute before realizing that it wouldn't be a go. All the same, I knew getting the first tenant was crucial—and Anaida was perfect. She had come to New York from Puerto Rico and did powerful, political paintings about violence against women, among other subjects. It was clear she had grit and soul and would bring an artistic spirit to the building that I wanted to encourage. It was at that moment that I had an idea.

"Listen," I said. "What if you didn't have to pay rent? What if we could do a trade instead?" After talking it through, she took me to her art showing in Harlem, and I was allowed to pick a piece off the wall. The one I chose was a colorful painting with spiral motifs, a pair of ghostly limbs and rich, deep colors; in exchange, I gave her free rent for a year. Of course, it meant that I would have to forego my own management fee of $12,000 to make up the difference, but to me, it was more than worth it. Sure enough, after breaking the ice with Anaida, Sidney and I were pulling in a slow trickle of other tenants.

Towards the end of the deal, there was still the rooftop billboard to deal with, which turned out to be more complicated than I thought. The way Ari and I had structured the deal was that we would have control of the billboard when the lease on it expired. Originally, it was leased to a public company called Entravision, and as part of the closing conditions, I insisted that we had to get a signature from the sign company that we owned it. After I got the signature we needed, Ari and I took over the billboard and got a better lease rate when the lease expired.

As our loans were close to coming due, we refinanced the building and were able to take out some of the capital we put in tax-free to redistribute to our investors—and as we did so, it became clear that Ari and I had gotten in a little above our heads on First Bronx. We had faced countless challenges and had learned a lot as a result, but it had come with a fair share of stumbles—among them underestimating the funds we needed to finish the deal. In the end, the margins we predicted were thinner than we thought they would be.

We had not profited the way we thought we would and had come closer to breaking even. All the same, our investors and close friends hadn't lost faith or been terribly disappointed. They had seen the scale of difficulties we'd taken on without flinching, as well as the high-quality product we had delivered at the end of it all. It may have been a learning experience, but Ari and I were just getting started.

Ari and I had always been great friends as kids, but it was a joy to discover that we loved working together as well —and on the heels of First Bronx, we found another opportunity not far away in the South Bronx closer to Fordham Road. The building was at 2337-79 Creston Avenue. It was a relic but still grand in its own right. It stood tall on the corner of 187th Street and needed some TLC but was generally in good shape for what it was.

The owners were an Albanian couple, though the wife was much more involved in running the building than the husband was. She was an attractive woman who could come down to the building all dressed up, going door to door collecting rents, which seemed outrageous to me. It was a rough block, and there she was, knocking doors in person! It was a prime example of what not to do as a landlord, but I didn't say anything.

Right away, the deal made sense: for people who didn't have deep pockets, the building was close to subways and shops. It was a mile up the road from Yankee Stadium, right off the Grand Concourse in the Bronx. The way real estate cycles in New York, a lot of those buildings end up becoming low-income occupied—all good, hard-working people, but people who tend not to have a lot of money. Even so, the area used to be considered the Champs-Elysée of the Bronx, and the buildings used to be magnificent. With a little love, I figured, we could do some of the legwork of restoring them to their former glory.

The incredible thing was it was a 52-unit building with five stores in it across from a turn-of-the-century middle school. Still, even though we'd come into an asset with a ton of upside, the renovations were going to be staggering—far more difficult than they'd been on First Bronx.

"We're going to have to syndicate it," I told Ari. Although we'd raised some money from friends and family to put First Bronx together, this was going to be on a much larger scale, with more investors and bigger checks—and Ari was uncomfortable with asking for so much money from people we knew.

"You can't think of it like they're doing us a favor," I told him. "We're offering them a real opportunity to grow their money. It has to be presented as a unique thing and an opportunity to invest with us, and then we'll bust our asses to provide them with an outsized return."

As I learned very quickly, raising money was as much of an art as renovating a classic building. Although Ari and I both had our fair share of connections to people with money in our network, it's not all that easy to sell a massive, decrepit building like the one we were selling. Instead, we had to paint a beautiful picture. We were selling the potential for tremendous upside, but we were also selling a confident friendship. We were asking investors to take a leap of faith on the strength of Ari's and my integrity. In countless meetings, we gave some version of the following proposition:

"I'm offering you an opportunity to join forces. We will work and create value for you from your money, and all you have to do is trust us to do it."

It was an important lesson in the psychology of truly successful people: they were willing to part with serious money if they could clear the trust barrier—in other words, as long as they trusted we were going to give their money back with interest. Earning that trust was something I took very seriously, and it was hard work.

The process of gathering investors took a long time and a lot of difficult conversations, but eventually, we put together 15 or 16 investors in the deal from our respective networks, many of whom also invested in First Bronx. Once again, we were asking family and friends like David Zarabi to put in money, some of whom were writing checks as large as $185,000—worth approximately ten percent of the entire deal. In all, we raised $1.85 million.

With so much going on, it was making less and less sense to keep working at Hartman & Craven, even if I had formed some good relationships from working there. One of my newer and growing friendships was with Eric Edidin, who was also getting antsy. Eric was married to one of Rachel's best friends, and we had become friends over our mutual heritage, love of Israel and our passion for business. Over the years, we'd had many deep conversations about raising children in a wholesome way and questioning the meaning of life. He had invested alongside other close friends on First and Second Bronx while building his CV at pedigreed Wall Street shops. One night, he came to my office to drink scotch and talk things over when the conversation came up organically.

"It feels like it's time to get out on my own," Eric said. "I've got the education, the experience and the network at this point to make a go at it. I think I want to set up my own credit hedge fund, but of course, I have my reservations."

"There's nothing stopping you, Eric," I told him, both of

us a little more spirited than usual. "You don't want to be stuck in one place forever, and you have everything you need to do it on your own." Even as I was saying it, I felt like I was really giving myself advice.

Around the same time, the litigation with Ruth was wrapping up as well. It had taken plenty of time, research and frustrating emails on my part, but I'd never had to go to court over it—the lawyers had handled everything. It was my first real taste of protracted litigation, and I couldn't deny how unpleasant the process had been even though I wasn't overly involved in the proceedings. The results were as expected: she lost everything, and I actually got offered the property back at half price. I didn't take it; I was just relieved to be done with the entire headache.

Soon after, Ari and I were wrapping up the renovations on Second Bronx and continuing to find tenants for it in early 2007 when I got another call from Eric. Sure enough, he had followed his gut (and my prodding) and had given his notice to start his own credit hedge fund called Archer Capital and was already having some success.

"Things are going so well over here," Eric told me on the phone. "You should come work with us. Forget about Hartman; let's start doing some deals!" As the conversation evolved, we discussed the possibility of forming a strategic partnership between my company Wilder Realty and Archer Capital. In general terms, the agreement was that I would hunt for good deals and bring them to Archer when one looked particularly promising. In exchange (and on deals they agreed to pursue), Archer would deliver access to equity capital and use their own balance sheet and reputation to help secure financing as necessary. The result of the trade was that we would share the profit participation we might take from investors in exchange for making a given deal work. It would marry my talent for sourcing deals with Archer Capital's analytics and fiscal backbone.

For a long time, I'd been tied to the security and prestige of a law career, even though I was getting tired of it. If I left to go work for Archer Capital, it would be a complete leap out of law and into finance and investing. It would be a clear break into the world of entrepreneurship, a leap I'd been ready to make for some time. I'd hesitated for a while, but everything had been going so well that there didn't seem to be any reason not to do it—all the past few deals I'd closed had been difficult, but they'd paid off tremendously.

At long last, I gave my notice. Ironically enough, right after I quit, two of my peers were appointed partners in the firm! I could tell they had done it so as not to lose anyone else, but I couldn't help but groan at the timing. Around the same time, Rachel and I got some major news: she was pregnant.

"No way," I said as she showed me the positive test in our apartment. She handed it over, and I stared at the plus in disbelief. As I looked up, I saw that Rachel was processing the same cocktail of euphoria and terror as I was.

"This is amazing," I said, hugging her and tearing up. "This is so amazing." Having children was always a part of our plan, and we were both nearly shaking with excitement. Next were questions: Who can we tell? How long should we wait? At last, I told her she would be an amazing mother, which brought on a whole new round of tears and celebration.

I was excited for a chance to flex my entrepreneurial

muscles at Archer, and I thought everyone would have the same appetite that I did. Once again, I found out very quickly that wasn't the case. The guys there had a much more institutional mindset than I was used to. The market was frothy, and they were very cautious about spending. The company did live trading, P/E deals and hard money loans, and right away, it was clear the level of sophistication and nuance in the deals was exponentially greater than what I was used to. At the beginning, a big part of my day-to-day was looking at spreadsheets that were making my eyes glaze over. The entire thing was draining, so I thought the best thing might be to hire an analyst to work the numbers for me.

I posted an ad on Craigslist, and sure enough, a young man named Tony Chen put in his resumé. Right away, Tony's sharp mind and mathematical insights impressed me —he had skills in that regard that outstripped my own. After conducting an interview that went well, I hired him to join me at Wilder Realty. Around the same time, my first cousin Shalom Yona (or Sho Yo, as I affectionately called him) introduced me to Steve Hackel, a close friend of his who, like him, was also a devout Jew from Long Island.

"Steve is very talented," my cousin told me. "If you're looking for another property manager or help with your business, you two should talk." It was true that I was looking for some help with management and deal sourcing, so I set up a meeting. Stepping out from Hartman & Craven midday, I met Steve in Midtown on the street, and we did a walk and talk.

As he explained, he was getting out of the hotel mini-bar business and wanted something more fulfilling and challenging. We went through his qualifications and talked about life and business, and right away, I could see his potential.

"My hope is to build a company," I told Steve. "A significant, multi-family real estate business that will keep growing. And as it grows, I want everyone involved to grow right along with it." After talking it through, it was clear he was sincere and eager about the vision I had, and I brought him onboard as well. After that, the best early decision I made was to have Tony create a series of spreadsheets that automatically generated spreadsheets for note deals Steve and I were looking at, based on the assumption parameters we supplied. It was essential because the level of financial and analytical detail the firm required for any deal it entered was significantly more difficult and thorough than I had been accustomed to.

Joel Fogel was head of real estate investing at Archer Capital, and as I got to know him, I could see what a precise and analytical guy he was. In many of my past deals, the initial decision to enter or not was based on instinct and what I'd always called back-of-the-napkin math. After that, there was always more detailed number-crunching and legal legwork to ensure everything looked good, but because Archer Capital took a more institutional approach, the decision-making process was slower and more deliberate.

As I learned, Joel and his team at Archer (along with any other institutional capital firm) had a way of modeling deals into upside, middle side and downside cases from the very beginning, before even considering a deal. Their way of analyzing things was to break down what a project's potential returns would look like if things went perfectly, if they went okay and if they went horribly—and if a given deal didn't automatically clear all three risk tiers in a way that made financial sense, it wouldn't pass. It was an invaluable approach and a lesson in how to get large-financing for large-scale projects.

The result of having Joel as a foil was that we closed very few deals, which was fairly frustrating. Steve and I would go out and hunt for properties we thought looked promising; after that, we would run the numbers through the financial analysis system Tony had set up. If it passed our system, we brought our work to Archer Capital and Joel's analysis team. More often than not, Joel's team would dig even deeper or project the deal even more stringently into the future. The result of that additional analysis was that most of the deals we initially thought were good were not strong enough opportunities for Archer to pursue.

The constant dialogue of deconstructing potential investments was stressful and antithetical to my personality in many ways, though I could still see the value in it. There was no detail too small and no risk too tangential for Joel and his team to catch and dissemble in wholly convincing ways. In our many spirited debates, sometimes we agreed on analysis and potential upside, and sometimes we did not; either way, we never proceeded with any deals unless everyone was on the same page.

Eventually, we found an opportunity in the Bronx on White Plains Road, a full block front of retail and residential. The place had been owned by an older Italian guy who hadn't had to work very hard to make money from it. As a result, there was an obvious element of neglect (or upside depending on who was looking)—things were beginning to fall apart, lease opportunities weren't being maximized, and the curb appeal was lost. The place had storefronts and was ripe for renovation and value creation, and the existing owner was willing to sell for $6.5 million.

We followed the process we always followed: after our initial research, we ran it through the system, evaluating the downside, middle case, and upside scenarios carefully. After it passed that, we double-checked our work and brought it to Archer, ready to be shot down. To our pleasant surprise, Joel and Eric ran it through their own models and came to the same conclusion we did: they concurred, it was a good opportunity! After many meetings and with Archer Capital's funding in the deal alongside my capital, we closed on it.

On the one hand, having Wilder Realty find an investment that passed institutional muster felt like a huge achievement and one that was long overdue—it proved just how far we had come in terms of our own sophistication and understanding of the market. Still, it had been a long road, and it was beginning to feel like our respective companies weren't a great fit for one another.

In truth, our scrappy approach of acquiring distressed real estate assets had never been a core part of Archer Capital's business since so much of the money they managed and lent out was institutional and operated at a greater scale than Wilder Realty did. The truth is, the frothy market conditions meant that we had entered into our joint venture at a suboptimal time: everything was overpriced relative to its actual value, and Archer Capital's entire team were savvy enough investors to know not to jump at bad deals, as were we.

No matter how frustrated I'd been about all the analysis paralysis at Archer Capital, I had learned a tremendous amount from Joel and his team. Though I valued my own outsider underdog status and considered that I might never fully embrace the institutional mindset, it was now another tool in our arsenal that my team and I could bring to bear on future projects. It was also true that the caution with which Archer Capital approached major investments turned out to be prudent because a year later, all the market optimism that had made everybody with a dollar to invest look like a genius had turned upside down entirely.

12

MAKING LEMONADE OUT OF LEMONS

On January 7, 2008, the day Rachel and I had been waiting for finally came: our beautiful daughter Zohar was born in Mount Sinai Hospital. Her name was chosen in homage to the *Zohar*, a foundational text in Jewish mysticism. In Hebrew, the name means "radiance," and as soon as we first laid eyes on her, she was all smiles and energized, so beautiful we knew her name suited her. On the way to the hospital, I called Ari and told him that Zohar was on her way. Even though he'd been vacationing in the Maldives, he dropped everything and went from puddle jumper to puddle jumper to make it back to New York City. Just a few hours after Zohar was born, Ari knocked on the hospital door with a million-watt smile and a bottle of scotch in his hand, the first of my close friends to hold my daughter.

I took a walk outside to get some air shortly after and breathed in deeply, full of exuberance. I'd been eager to greet my daughter and was excited to be a father, but nothing could've prepared me for seeing her for the first time. The love I felt was overwhelming. My whole life, I'd taken risks without fear for how it might affect me, but something in that calculus had now changed. I was no longer just thinking about myself. I had to think about the safety of my family and how I would provide for them. I'd always wanted to do more and do better for myself in business, but now I was infused with new inspiration. I wanted more and better from life for my family—and I would soon get my chance to meet that challenge.

Everyone has their own version of finding out about the market crash on October 24, 2008. Plenty of us probably remember seeing the opening bell on whatever news network we watched. It started 100 points or so down, then another 50. At its worst that day, the market was down a whopping 777 points before settling around 450. It was the dot-com bubble popping all over again, except this time it was even worse.

I remembered the pain of Building Brokers going under and how so much optimism had suddenly vanished overnight. Still, this time, my experience of the market crashing was completely different. Whenever you get bad news in life, there's the initial negative shock—but in this case, that fear and anxiety transmuted almost instantly into something else. Compared to the tenderness bordering on terror I felt for my daughter's safety, financial turbulence was nothing. I was calm.

Nobody had planned for the market crash, and I hadn't planned to feel the way I did. From being on the other side of it before, I knew just how painful and punishing it would be for plenty of people. Still, because of the recent successes I'd had and the deliberate choices I'd made to build my skills and launch on my own, I felt like I could see the matrix behind everything. From a capitalist perspective, I knew that the hardest times—like those ones we were sure to be entering—were when the greatest value would be created. It was value the right person could capture by being prepared, and I was prepared to capture it for my family. The easy and safe thing to say is that I was afraid and anguished when the market crashed. The truth was that given everything I'd come through and the preparations I'd made, it was a captivating and enlivening moment.

On a deep level, finding things that were distressed or that were deemed untouchable, pouring my energy and expertise into them and turning them around to create enormous value for myself, my friends and my family was what I was born to do. Part of the American Dream is that you can always reinvent yourself, and that's true in how the American financial system works as well. By way of example, bankruptcy has a very bad reputation and sounds like a scary thing, but in my eyes and as a result of my financial and legal education, I also saw it as a beautiful thing in certain circumstances. It meant that you could take an asset or a series of decisions that were sinking, non-performing or corrupted in some way and cut a deal to wipe the slate clean and start over again from scratch. By pulling the right financial and legal levers, a company or individual could wipe out indebtedness, rebuild and rise again.

I don't remember exactly where I was when I got the news about the 2008 subprime mortgage crisis or what the most important things were that happened in the following few months. What I do remember are the conversations I had with Harry Zubli about it. Harry and I went as far back as I did with David and Ari. We had gone to private school together as children, where we were both constantly getting into trouble for doing things like taping live M80s to jars filled with fireflies.

He was even wilder than I was in high school and grew to become a hustler just like I was. He had a law practice that dealt with foreclosures, and a lot of his business had been focused on buying distressed assets and non-performing debts specifically. It was in his blood, and he was great at it. We had talked before about working together over the years; in truth, it was a conversation that spanned decades. Since the market had fallen off a cliff, Harry had gone underwater on some of his personal real estate investments and wanted to talk through his options. Though from a certain perspective, it seemed like terrible news, I knew the time for us to work together had finally arrived.

"Danny, I'm invested in a sizable Vegas land deal that is falling apart," he said. "I'm in over my head here—I'm ducking banks at this point." Because I'd known Harry my whole life, I knew he wasn't someone who made rash decisions or who was irresponsible. On the contrary, he was one of the coolest, calmest thinkers I had ever met. Harry had a brilliant legal mind and had himself a great business. If the economic crash could damage him, it could damage anyone.

As he explained, one bank was giving him problems, and he didn't know how to proceed. Knowing Harry, I considered how fortunate I was to be in the position of giving advice to someone so accomplished and wise on his own—but I also knew how easily the situation could be reversed (and would be over the years of our friendship).

"The first thing to do is not panic," I said. "Once you've

calmed down, the next thing is to look at your situation for what it is and clean up the toxicity. Don't dodge the calls from the banks—take the calls and settle with them. We will figure this out together, and you will come out clean and even stronger than you were before."

Though I was trying to be uplifting, the advice I had given about taking a short-term loss was something Harry didn't want to hear. "How can I do that?" he asked. "I'm going to lose control of multiple assets. I'll be down so much money. This toxicity is going to spread to my good stuff as well."

"I'm telling you, Harry, work with them to settle and get rid of anything you can that's going to stop you from growing," I said. "It will be a blow to your ego and a blow financially, but you want to get rid of those toxic files because there's going to be a lot of positivity in the time ahead. There are going to be a lot of opportunities for us to work together, and I think it's finally the right time."

After speaking to Harry, I knew I had to part ways with Archer Capital as soon as possible. I had learned a lot, greatly expanded my knowledge of finance and real estate and fostered some deep bonds, but their train moved too slowly for my taste, and all the red tape was constraining. My gut told me if I kept waiting around for the proper time and attention, I was going to end up working at McDonald's (and not in their acquisitions department). I had always been the kind of person who wanted to run into burning buildings rather than away from them, and those were exactly the market conditions of 2008. I needed to grab my board and get in the water because the set was here.

Although many new things were going on, the reality

was I'd left a relatively safe stream of income to go work free-lance and live off the money coming in from my independent investments. Despite the risks, I couldn't have been more excited. Harry and I had been talking about going into business for over a decade, and now, his expertise and mine were lining up perfectly. Harry was an expert in foreclosures and complex legal work, which I wanted little part of, whereas I had the strategic mind and the moxie to turn around even the most problematic investments. It was a combination that gave us the confidence to go after some big deals. We were ready to reach out to banks about buying non-performing debt off their books, debt that they were aching to offload.

The first deal we looked closely at was a $1.2 million non-performing banknote on a property on Daly Avenue, right next to the Bronx Zoo. It was a 27-unit walk-up brown-stone, and the note was accruing at a 24 percent default rate; in fact, it had already accrued to $1.6 million. For that time, it was a big ticket for us to write. Most relatively small-time investors at that time were either bone dry or financially underwater, and we were no exception. Even so, I knew the upside on it was too good to pass up. We would have to make it work, one way or another.

Note deals were a significantly different undertaking than buying existing income-producing properties and reno-vating or adding value to them. On a note deal, what we were buying was ownership of the legal document outlining the mortgage agreement between a lender (a bank or other financial institution) and a borrower (the person or entity controlling the property). On distressed assets—of which there were many in 2008—the notes were essentially worth-less to the banks holding them because the borrowers couldn't make their payments. Worse, in fact, they were a liability that affected a bank's credit with their lender, namely the FED (because yes, banks have credit scores too).

In a typical situation that worked for both parties, the borrower would make monthly payments to the bank for whatever the term of the mortgage was, generally for five, seven, 10 or more years. After paying off the sum of the mortgage plus interest accrued, the note would be dissolved, and the asset would no longer be encumbered.

In essence, a home or a piece of commercial real estate serves as collateral for a bank when issuing a mortgage; if the borrower stops paying, the lender has the right to foreclose and take the asset. Still, foreclosing on assets and buildings is not something most (if any) banks want to be in the business of doing for many reasons. For one thing, taking properties from borrowers means holding those assets until they can be filled or sold, during which time banks accrue property taxes, operational expenses and other liabilities (whether the properties are vacant or occupied). For another thing, the foreclosure process is a complex and painful legal procedure that costs a ton of money to prosecute and is outside the core business of a bank (namely, borrowing and lending money).

Finally, one of the best-kept secrets of the banking industry is that upon initiating the foreclosure process, banks are also required to report the associated loan as a Non-Performing Asset (NPA)—and holding too many NPAs on their books hurts their credit rating and their ability to borrow money from the Federal Reserve or even remain solvent. It meant that for a bank holding many NPAs, their best options were often to pressure the borrower into making payments again (which was generally a futile endeavor during bad times) or to sell their debt at a discount and cut their losses.

Smaller shops with the right legal expertise like us could acquire those notes, pursue the foreclosure to completion and take total control of the asset, or else simply accrue double-digit returns on the interest that was owed and get paid off with outsized yields. Because we were nimbler on our feet than a nationwide bank, we could then sell any assets we acquired outright at court-directed auction for a lump sum payment, or we could restructure and reposition the properties and sell or hold them as we saw fit. On the other hand, another benefit was that we could acquire the distressed notes, borrow against them (which is known as note-on-note financing) and refinance them to take out our initial equity investment.

The legal legwork was extensive and involved looking through ownership history, outstanding mortgages, liens, rights and so on to ensure our title was "clean" and that the asset would pass smoothly into our hands after foreclosure. Even after foreclosing successfully, there were often countless violations to clear and related issues to fix. We still had to add value somehow, just as we had to when buying a real asset. In my view, distressed notes were the most attractive risk-adjusted asset within their asset class because if due diligence was done correctly, all the potential outcomes were clearly defined: you either got paid off and earned double-digit returns, or you foreclosed and captured the collateral (to sell, finance or hold for long term appreciation). In either case, the resulting returns far outweighed the associated risks.

For those with a stomach for risk and a mind for byzantine legal details, it was an aggressive strategy with the potential for high returns. On top of those challenges, getting access to a bank's list of assets came with its own complexities—and since we didn't have enough of our own capital to invest (you never do if you are continually growing your book), we would have to borrow money or bring equity investors to enter any deals we might pursue.

On Daly Avenue, the first thing Harry and I did was reach into our immediate network for a private lender or investor. Through his synagogue, Harry knew an investor named Tzion who had money to lend and or invest, but he and his colleagues also knew they had all the leverage in the situation. In a sense, he had a scrappy immigrant attitude that I understood all too well: *we'll invest this money, but it's going to cost you.*

When everything had been settled, they gave us most of the money we needed between equity and financing they lent us—but at 70 percent of the profits plus a preferred 10 percent return on their loans, it had been expensive. For our part, Harry and I put in about 10 percent of the total deal ourselves. The entire arrangement meant that on the 10 percent equity we owned in the deal, we kept all of the profit—but on the rest, we retained 30 percent of the profits after paying off the interest and the loans.

Despite the difficult personalities we were dealing with, it was clear that flipping distressed debt was the business to be in. After closing on financing and having Harry spearhead the foreclosure process, the borrower ended up selling the building and had to pay us in full—including all the default interest and accruals. Even despite the unfavorable financial terms we entered into, Harry and I turned a handsome profit and were ready to rinse and repeat.

It was becoming clear to me right away that buying and selling distressed debt was like strapping yourself to a rocket engine. Although the preparation required for a note deal was as difficult and painstaking as it was for a renovation project, the return on sweat equity was so much higher than buying a property or finishing a busted project. To be successful, it was essential to work with a great legal team to suss out all the details and complexity of any given deal—because even the slightest error in diligence could be terminal to the paper and our ability to get paid off with full accruals. As I learned, there was a lot you could learn about how a deal would go by looking at the borrower's file and reading between the lines.

When it came to banks, their reasons for not aggressively pursuing foreclosures made sense (even if it was sometimes difficult to explain to potential investors). On the other side of the equation, why a borrower would stop paying their mortgage was a more complex question. In the 2008 crash, millions of residential homeowners couldn't afford to make payments through relatively little fault of their own; while the same was also true for commercial real estate owners, the factors and fundamentals that went in were different.

After doing the research, sometimes it became obvious that the owner held other buildings that they valued more, so they let one of the assets fall into neglect. On Daly Avenue, Harry and I found that the borrower had been paying an extra one percent in interest to the bank all because he hadn't done some administrative fixes at his building—fixes that would've been so simple to make! Though one percent may not sound like much, a smart real estate investor would know that one percent compounding interest on a sizeable loan made an enormous difference in profits and relative safety as an owner. The only kind of person who wouldn't pursue such a simple fix had to be very busy, very lazy or asleep at the wheel; it was a great tell-tale sign.

As Harry and I pursued more and more notes, we settled into our roles nicely. I hunted the deals, Harry oversaw the mental gymnastics and paperwork of complex foreclosures, we strategized on the best approach and I morphed into a conductor once the deal was in play. But while a smooth note deal could help investors avoid the pains of renovation and dealing with tenants, there were still significant risks and traps that you could fall into.

In 2010, I sourced a distressed note on a 54-unit elevator-equipped apartment building in the Bronx at 2285 Sedgwick Avenue. I found it on a Capital One bank sheet of non-performing loans. Capital One was a shit show at the time, buried in non-performing mortgages and selling them to anyone who had the funds. They were holding so many bad notes that they did not even know what was in their portfolio; they were merely assigning all of it in batches to low-level, inexperienced employees being paid to offload their inventory. Essentially, Capital One was having a fire sale (like a garage sale of notes only we could review all the treasures right off a spreadsheet), and we were benefitting.

To begin, I negotiated with Capital One about their note. They were owed $3.25 million, but after back and forth, I was able to negotiate a purchase price of $1.8 million. As great as this was, I was facing my recurring problem: lack of funding. With so much fear in the market, money was very expensive to borrow—and the prospect of investing in something that wasn't performing could be tricky to explain and hard to stomach. We needed to meet better and more efficient sources of financing if we were going to succeed.

After a meeting with a young broker named Sharone Sohayegh, I was introduced to Stanley Gallant from Galster Funding. We met to discuss the opportunity, and I explained how much financing I would need to move forward. We talked everything through, and at some point, he was satisfied and ready to move forward. I could follow his reasoning: though we were asking for a lot, he knew his value was protected because I was still investing money in front of him —not to mention the building was worth way more than what I would be paying for the building's debt. In essence, I would be the one doing all the grunt work and taking on most of the risk—and if I couldn't deliver, he would be the first one in line to clean up the mess I'd left behind at a cost basis of $33,000 per door—absolutely dirt cheap for Bronx apartments. At the end of our meeting, I had a handshake deal from Stanley to fund the entire $1.8 million if I could provide a rent roll and clean title.

With the funding in place, I took $327,000 out of my account to fund the taxes, prepaid interest for the note on note financing and other closing costs on the note—roughly every cent I had in the world at the time. Though I knew my money would be paid back in multiples, I had always been programmed not to sink everything into just one deal. To mitigate my risk and to offer my friends some of the upside, I then syndicated equity in the deal among friends and fellow investors, including Steve. David Zarabi came into the deal as well, and as an added wrinkle, I arranged for David Zarabi to loan Harry the money for his portion of the equity, which he would later pay back to David. After everything was done, I retained 20 percent of the equity in the deal—but because I had structured the syndication as a profit share, I also retained 30 percent of the profits from the investor pool as well (my ROSE).

As we'd gotten control of the note, the next steps were to foreclose on the owner to get control of the actual building. It meant the borrower would have to either sell the asset or refinance, lest we win back his collateral. The current owner had held it for two-and-a-half decades and now owed the bank $3.25 million—and since he was out of the money, he was also accruing default interest that we were entitled to at a rate of 24 percent a year. If he did not sell or refinance quickly, he would rack up an additional $780,000 a year in debt. I reasoned that rather than having Harry pursue the entire foreclosure process and take it back from him through a protracted court battle, I could meet with him to try and buy the deed directly. When the time came for me to meet with him to discuss what he wanted for the deed, he forcefully threw out the round number of $750,000.

"Forget it!" I said bluntly and in kind. "You have 2,000 violations on this building with the city of New York. On top of that, your heat is flickering on and off in the middle of winter, and your tenants are going ballistic!" I knew that if he sold his deed to us, we would be dealing with a major mess, but again, all I could see was potential. Regardless of my inner dialogue or my cavalier approach to the negotiations, none of the details mattered that day because he didn't want to sell. Instead, he wanted me out of his building.

Soon after that, there was a five-alarm fire at the building, and two of the ground-level units were destroyed. An investigation revealed that one of the tenants had been using his apartment as a prayer center, and there were lit candles everywhere—a blatant violation of the terms of his lease. Even so, NYC's socialist-leaning housing legislation made it nearly impossible to evict a tenant, short of them murdering someone in the unit (though even then, you would have a tough time). As a result of that fire, the gas provider Con Edison shut off service to the entire building. Clearly, the noose around the owner's neck was tightening. His building was now without heat, water and cooking gas in the middle of an unforgiving New York City winter, and his tenants were joining forces to engage in a full-scale revolt. Adding fuel to the fire, the *Daily News* had plastered a full page spread with a photo of the building, complete with irate tenants hanging their sheets out the windows with messages painted on them with slogans like "NO HEAT," "NO HOT WATER" and "ARREST THE LANDLORD." The rest of the media joined in the schadenfreude, and soon enough, my phone started ringing.

"Daniel, we're going to lose everything on this!" David said. He was into our deal for about 25 percent of the equity, so I understood his panic—on the surface, this looked like the worst thing ever. But I knew it wasn't.

"David, just relax and wait," I told him. "This is the best possible thing that could've happened to us." I knew a situation this bad was bound to turn into a PR opportunity for the entire local leadership in New York. I also figured that this might create an opportunity for leverage against the deadbeat landlord who didn't want to sell his debt to us. Sure enough, I got another call the next day—this time, from the Bronx congressman's assistant.

"What the hell is going on over on Sedgwick Avenue?" he asked. Clearly, his office wanted to get right down to business. "There are 200 people without heat and hot water, and we need to get this resolved immediately."

"I completely agree; let's get it resolved," I said. "The only problem is I can't help here—I don't have control over the building, so I don't have the legal right to fix the underlying issues and help your constituents. If I did have that right, of course, I would fix it immediately, but I'm just the bank in this situation."

There was a beat of silence on the other end. "I don't think you understand," the assistant said. "Someone is going to jail here."

"It's not going to be me because I have no control over the building," I said. "I understand the seriousness of this situation, but my hands are tied—again, I am just the bank here. I suggest that your office apply pressure to the owner. Tell him that if he does not remedy the building issues swiftly, the consequences will be dire." Once I hung up with the assistant, I immediately called Harry.

"Harry, I just got off the phone with the congressman's office, and they're out for blood," I said. "We need to call his attorney and tell him there's a serious situation here. Tell him that the congressman's office is gunning for his client and that if they know what's good for them, they'll meet with me as soon as possible—and tell them to come with humble expectations." Harry made the call, and soon enough, we had another meeting set up, this time at his office.

This time, the owner had brought his daughter-in-law

over, and the entire story behind the building's decline quickly snapped into place. His daughter-in-law had been running the building, and she didn't know the first thing about real estate. It should not have come as a surprise that she had run the place into the ground. I pointed out the many issues the building faced and offered him a check for $50,000 to give us the deed—and before long, he was shouting at me again from across his coffee table.

The truth about foreclosures, particularly on a large commercial scale, was plain enough to see in that moment. Even if this man had made a serious mistake by letting his daughter-in-law run the building, and even if he was being a terrible steward of his building and the people in it, it was still a very painful and emotional situation for him. He was clearly in duress like many other Americans were at that time. Taking assets away from delinquent borrowers was always a highly unpleasant situation—people's sweat and tears had often been poured into developing those assets over the years. For others, taking that asset away could amount to taking away their life's work. In light of all that, I had to show him that I was offering a way out and a way to ease his pain— no matter how much fury he threw my way.

"You need to see this situation for what it is," I told him calmly. "I'm getting this building one way or another, and the way this is going now, you're going to end up in jail. Is that what you want?"

He was quiet, so I continued.

"You're completely underwater on an asset that is spiraling out of your control," I said. "What I'm offering is a lot lower than what you're asking, but I'm not trying to pour salt in your wounds. You've made a lot of money off this building for a long time, and now there's no upside left for you. It's all headaches and costs ahead, and if you're not even collecting rent from your tenants, you won't have the funds you need to improve the building before the authorities come to take you away for criminal neglect. So let me buy the deed from you. I'll handle all the issues from here on out. You'll be out of the hot seat, and all your problems will be over." After thinking it over in furious silence for a minute, he agreed.

His problems might have been over, but mine were just beginning.

Immediately, I faced the wrath of a mass of angry tenants with neglected apartments that had no heat or hot water. These were Bronx tenants—which is to say that they were not inclined to take any shit from bad management; if I didn't fix things quickly, there was no telling what might happen. I started by looking at the insurance policy I had taken out when I bought the note. Although these exchanges are typically associated with borrowers' insurance, I had the foresight to add my own additional force-placed policy when we bought any note. I was never so grateful for insurance as I was at that moment.

After reading through the contract very closely, Steve Hackel and I found an obscure and often overlooked section that talked about law and ordinance coverage. It said that if a casualty occurred in the apartments and the municipality made a proclamation that the building needed to be restored to meet new building codes, the insurance company would pay for it. I had to do a double take. When Con Edison came to turn off the gas lines, they noted that the lines were not compliant with the current codes, and they shut off *all* the gas lines, not just the top two. In other words, the lines required restoration, and the local municipality had said so. My initial objective in reading the contract had been solely to ensure that we had coverage for the two units that had to be gutted due to fire, but this clause meant that we were entitled to far more.

Together, Steve and I submitted the claim to the insurance company and fought for our argument in painstaking detail. In the calls that ensued, Steve was a fierce adversary—he crushed the negotiations, and in the end, the insurance company agreed to abide by their policy. The result was rather than just paying for those two units and their old gas lines, the insurance company had to pay for the entire building's gas lines to be upgraded, a whopping $230,000 insurance recovery of which I only spent a fraction. Despite the huge win, I was still dealing with a building full of incredibly pissed-off Bronx tenants, who were among the most resourceful. Over my years working buildings in the Bronx, I had built up admiration and respect for them—most of these tenants were very good people, just with limited dollars. I knew I had to do something to restore morale to avoid a full mutiny. Working out of a tiny office, I gathered the two or three people I had working for me to help and told them the plan.

"Listen, these people are angry and legitimately so; the prior owner had no respect for their wellbeing, and now their holiday season is about to be ruined," I said. "What I want you to do is buy 60 Thanksgiving turkeys from Boston Market. We're going to hand them out in the lobby on Thanksgiving."

On Thanksgiving, the three of us got bundled up and stood shivering in the lobby, handing out turkeys to a building full of furious tenants. In all, the gesture cost us about $6,000, and though it didn't land as well as I'd hoped with the tenants—who can blame them, in all honesty—it did earn us a few meager points, and the situation was back under control. Above all, it was simply the right thing to do given everything they had been through.

After settling the chaos, refinancing the building and taking out $3 million to fix everything up and take some cash out, the market gradually started to turn towards the positive —and all kinds of investors and lenders started chasing our price upward. Someone came with an offer to buy it for $4 million; then another came with an offer for $5 million! Even so, we were patient and didn't sell. We had equity in a great building that was appreciating year after year and planned to hold it for a long time (much later, in 2017, we sold the building to a family for $8.5 million on a 1031 exchange, like my father had done with the chicken coop, and leveraged the asset into another building in Chinatown).

While I had a love for all the other parts of real estate development and ownership, it was clear that finding smart angles on distressed debt was the lever that would propel my team, my friends and I further and further towards our financial dreams. With our combined legal and financial skill sets and our determined attitude, we were in our groove—and the deals we were taking on were getting bigger and bigger.

13

THE BIRTH OF BH3

As Harry and I got into our groove, we took on more and more distressed notes and were becoming increasingly effective at flipping them for profit. There was one on Suffolk Street, a deal that was almost overlooked on a bank sheet that made us over a million dollars in less than 60 days on a $200,000 investment. There was a note on 125th Street in Harlem, a note on 7th in Harlem, one on 187th Street in Inwood and another on Jamaica Avenue. All were voluminous and required ongoing negotiations with banks, scrambles to raise funds and aggressive foreclosures (complemented by our general willingness to work with the borrowers on simultaneous tracks).

On a note on 187th Street, Steve cut his teeth when the banker told him he was going to sell to someone else for $25,000 more and would be closing the following week. I told him to put the banker on hold.

"In the future, do you want to complain about how this banker screwed you over?" I asked him. "Or would you rather still get this deal done?" He replied that he still wanted to get it done, so I suggested that he tell the banker that we would pay $25,000 above his offer if we could close the following day. The banker agreed, and we worked overnight to raise the approximately $1.8 million we needed. It was such a scramble that one investor who owned a shoe business sent his certified check the next morning in a sedan via car service for us to grab and quickly deposit in time for us to close.

After leaving Maidman & Mittelman, I had stayed in touch with the family and often went to their functions. I remained friends with Mitchel Maidman and used to bullshit with him all the time, and because he was so brilliant, I would ask him for legal advice from time to time. At the same time, I was searching for new distressed debt opportunities and found one that I thought Mitchel and I would be perfect partners for.

The deal was a $13.5 million note from New York Community Bank, which was collateralized by 303 apartments and eight stores in the Bronx, spread across eight buildings. I knew the deal was a great opportunity, but also that it required some significant financial connections. Fortunately, the Maidman family had incredible rapport with banks all around New York City—and for his part, Mitchel understood stabilized housing as well as anyone in the city, so it was a natural fit.

Because Mitchel essentially had carte blanche at New York Community Bank, he spearheaded the negotiations with the bank while I sourced the deal. It became clear that we would need to do note-on-note financing, which I was not keen on doing. The loan we were taking out required that we sign personal guarantees worth eight or nine million dollars. Although Mitchel was a big boy with many assets at the time, it was a level of risk and personal liability that I wasn't entirely comfortable taking on. I told Mitchel as much when he finally turned to me and sighed.

"Daniel, shut the fuck up," he said. "Hold your nose and sign the papers." Ultimately, it made me laugh, as he often did. Mitchel was right—it was a lot of risk for where I was in my career, but the upside was worth it. Even beyond the financing, all the arrangements of the deal were convoluted. The borrower was a group of young guys who were completely underwater—but behind the scenes, the person who sold them the building was a guy named Frank Palazzolo, an Italian guy from New York who at one time was rated one of the top 10 slumlords in the city.

As we unraveled the details of the deal, we realized that Frank still had entire control of the deal rather than these young guys. The reason for this was because Frank had made these guys sign silent second mortgages and personal guarantees that were theoretically worth millions, but what it really meant was that he was at the helm. As a result of this curious nuance, it was clear we would have to negotiate with Frank. The first person to meet with Frank was Harry, after which I got a phone call.

"Daniel, this guy has shark eyes," Harry said, clearly somewhat shaken. "You feel like he would kill you without a second thought and never think of it again." I knew Harry to be an incredibly calm and collected person, rarely off-put, so I was a bit surprised.

"Come on, Harry," I said. "What are you talking about? He's just a businessman."

"I'm serious," Harry insisted. "Just be aware when you talk to him."

Later on, Mitchel and I set up a meeting with Frank at the Trump Westchester. As usual, I was ready to find any kind of collaborative and cooperative angle possible to make things go smoothly as possible—but I could see what Harry meant. From the beginning, it was clear that Frank had the personality of an honest criminal—not because he was doing anything illegal, but because he did not care to hide how unscrupulous he was. He just said whatever was on his mind.

"So you guys want to push this into bankruptcy," he said to us. "That's no problem, but you can't do shit unless I cooperate. So pay me $1.5 million for the deeds. The kids you're talking to have no control. I have all the control here." It was hilarious how outrageous and brazen he was being, but I appreciated how transparent he was about who he was. Of course, we would not sign any guarantees despite a request from him to do so on some fresh notes, but after more negotiation, we agreed to give him the $1.5 million in exchange for a cooperative bankruptcy workout. In the process of doing all that, we took over the buildings as the mortgagee in possession during the foreclosure and starting cleaning house— conventional lenders would not want to do that because there was way too much liability, but we didn't care. Because Mitchel and I were nimbler than a huge institution, we could take on more risk in exchange for greater upside, which we were more than happy to do.

After hunting down and buying several distressed debt deals, I had established good relationships with a number of banks that were all making each subsequent deal smoother.

Tony was doing an excellent job managing all technical and financial aspects of our business at Wilder Realty, while Steve was a brilliant mind and a bulldog who was just as ready to get in the trenches as I was. For a while, my management office was my used Range Rover, and on Sundays, Steve and I would drive around the Bronx fixing headaches at our buildings and putting rent bills on doors when necessary. Money was flowing in well off of a string of successes, and I was getting antsy again. I wanted to expand even further, so I looked for bigger and better opportunities. Meanwhile, Zohar was growing older, and in late 2008, Rachel was growing tired of New York City.

"We need room to grow and stretch out," Rachel said one day. "This city is so crowded and stressful as a place to raise children. We need to move—think Mediterranean lifestyle."

Initially, I frowned at the idea of leaving the city. I had a handful of great deals under my belt and enough money to put towards some fresh projects. Rachel and I discussed moving to Israel, but the compromise we landed on was Florida—it had palm trees and more of our fellow tribesmen, even if it was not quite the real thing (there is no place on the planet like Israel – truly the land of milk and honey). I was reluctant at first, but the more I thought of it, the more a change of scenery started to make sense. The recession had seriously impacted New York real estate, but the way it had throttled the market in Florida was an entirely different beast. If ever there was a golden opportunity to invest in distressed assets, clean it up my way with my partners and make enormous returns, it was now. Stressful though it might be to set up in a new city, my fire was lit, the challenge was exhilarating, and it was the best thing for my family. *Besides,*

I thought, *Rachel and I have both always been open to new challenges.*

Even though the idea of moving seemed great, I had built up a great network in New York and, with it, much momentum in my business. I would need to connect with Florida-based investors and businesspeople to know more about the area before doing anything drastic. I asked Joel Fogel, my counterpart at Archer Capital, if he knew anyone in Florida. With his recommendations and others, I put together a list of 10 to 12 "good guys" with whom to meet. I flew down to Florida a few times to meet people, and on one occasion, I brought my father with me because I wanted to take him on a vacation as a gesture of appreciation. It was on that trip that I met Greg Freedman.

My dad and I were sitting in the lobby of the Sagamore Hotel in South Beach when Greg walked up. My dad got up to leave, but Greg stopped him.

"Where's your dad going?" Greg asked. I told him he was just going to take a walk while we had a meeting.

"There's no need for that," he said. "Let's all hang out!"

We sat down together, and before long, we weren't talking about business at all, but rather about our backgrounds, our families, my father's history and life in general. Greg was smart, young, aggressive, straightforward—completely no-bullshit—which was hard to find. Our meeting went on for at least a few hours and flowed naturally, but it still seemed over all too soon. Even my dad was impressed—of everyone I'd met in Florida, Greg was the guy I'd liked the most. Some of the other people had made sense on paper in one or two ways, but the connection with Greg was effortless and natural.

I flew back to New York and started planning for our move, but I continued looking at Florida properties primarily through debt and came across an opportunity in Miami Beach that seemed promising. It was a partially completed 117-unit condominium complex right on the beach. The property was at 6000 Collins Avenue in Miami, a gorgeous part of the city resting between Collins Avenue and Indian Creek, right by the beach. After learning that the property note was held by Regions Bank, I started working angles there. The banker was not overly fond of Yankees like me, but I persisted in calling him even more than his wife did. A few months had passed since I'd met with Greg, and I thought I would give him a call to see if I could get any help on the deal.

"Hey, Greg, it's Daniel," I said. "I'm working on a debt deal on 6000 Collins in Miami, and there are a few things I can't figure out."

Immediately, Greg knew which property I was referring to, and it turned out he had been working it from his own angles as well. "I know everything about that deal," he replied. "What do you want to know?" I loved his confidence, but I wanted to know it was backed up by moxie.

"Don't waste your time," Greg said. "I tried working with the bank to get the note and couldn't get anywhere. They've been in and out of contract. It's an old boys club that's tough to get into."

"I've got a good relationship with Regions, and I've been hammering them," I replied, "so I have a deal lined up to buy the debt, but I want to see if I can work something out with the developer simultaneously to avoid a prolonged foreclosure."

"Let me get them on a conference call," Greg replied. Not 10 seconds later, he had Charlie Sieger on the phone, one of the most prominent architects in South Florida. By the end of the call, we had set up an in-person meeting. We had barely started working together, but I was already impressed by Greg's efficiency and dynamism.

The architect, general contractor and developer on that project were Charlie Sieger, Jose Suarez and their partner Ronnie Bloom, respectively. Charlie Sieger and Jose Suarez were the heads of one of the most prolific architectural firms in South Florida, Sieger Suarez. They were starchitects who had designed 35 or more of the most beautiful buildings in the region and were well known for their taste and business acumen. Unfortunately, on this project, they were facing imminent foreclosure.

As I had experienced over the years, foreclosures were often ugly. The plan on the deal was to buy about $45 million in debt, plus all the accruals—more than $60 million in value for what would cost us about $19 million. The project was around 400,000 square feet, 199,000 of which was net salable, finished real estate that was absolutely gorgeous. Priced out, it meant that we were getting beach-front condominiums for $84 per square foot, which, given South Florida prices, was practically theft. It would hurt their ego pretty badly to part with a project of that scale, and we knew it. With that in mind, we tried to approach them with compassion.

When Greg and I walked into Charlie Sieger and Jose Suarez's offices, everyone was a little on edge. Our goal was to earn their trust, so we took things slow to feel each other out first before getting to business. Soon enough, it became clear that Charlie had a natural gift for gab and was a creative beacon who loved to design, while Jose was more of a salt-of-the-earth personality who was centered and practical. As they explained, they had been partners for over 40 years. Once we had all gotten to know one another, it was time to get to the business at hand.

"We're getting calls non-stop," Jose said. As he explained, many opportunistic investors were looking to buy their debt and press them as aggressively as possible.

"It's like the vultures are descending on us," Charlie said. "We're getting threats that they're going to come after our own personal guarantees. I'm building up a legal team to sue the bank over this. The whole thing is a mess." As we listened, I could tell Greg's wheels were spinning just like mine were. We could certainly also be classified as opportunistic investors in this situation as well, but we had no interest in pinning anyone's back to the wall; in the context of this deal, that would just be poor gamesmanship. From an investing perspective, even if Jose and Charlie were out of the money and subject to personal guarantees, with the kind of legal defense they could mount, their case was liable to stretch on for years and years. Aside from the fact that taking an aggressive tack here would be like kicking someone while they were down, it also didn't make any sense from a business perspective.

"Guys, look," I said. "We're not interested in going after your personal guarantees. We can find a way to do this so it works out for everyone." Greg picked up on my lead and jumped in.

"You two have a long history of successful projects and incredible work between you," Greg said. "This situation has emerged from a marketplace that completely collapsed, and we're not here to make it worse."

"What we need you to understand is that we're not the bad guys here," I said. "We can stave off the bad guys." Though we hadn't worked together before, I noticed immediately that Greg and I were so in sync in the negotiations that it felt like magic. In the flow of the conversation, sometimes he had the control and rapport, and sometimes I did, but we were never getting tangled or in one another's way. In a high-pressure situation like this one, having someone who could give and take and pivot on a moment's notice was invaluable.

After some back and forth, Charlie explained how the original design for the building had come about and how much it meant to him. The unique low-rise profile of the building was born out of necessity when the land was down-zoned; all the same, it gave the project a unique feel. Greg and I listened intently before chiming back in.

"We're not here to pour salt in your wounds," I said. "We're interested in one thing: coming in and completing this project. You started this, and we want to finish it with you, together. Our goal is to create a cooperative situation we can all benefit from." Even if Jose and Charlie were esteemed architects turned developers of South Florida real estate, the legal and financial situation they found themselves in was enough to strike fear and skepticism into the heart of any developer. Even so, they could see from our approach that we sincerely cared about collaboration and about the value they had already created.

We impressed on them just how passionate we were about reinvigorating distressed assets and finding win-win situations. They opened up and explained how precarious their financial situation was, but we let them know that we were willing to step into it right along with them. We weren't negotiating across the table from them; we were on the same side.

After a few hours of discussion, we outlined an arrangement to keep them involved as consultants and assured them that we would not go after their personal guarantees. As Charlie and Jose realized we had no interest in humiliating them and that we would be giving them cash flow when they needed it most, we all shook hands, and they agreed to cooperate however they could. In a week or so, we had worked out a deal. While the negotiations were ongoing, Greg asked me privately how we would proceed.

"How do you want to do this?" he said. "Should I be a consultant? Should my team jump in?"

Both of us were feeling around in the dark a little bit since we didn't know each other well, but in light of the high-caliber conversations we'd already had, what Greg was suggesting showed a level of humility that was almost comical. It was admirable and reflected the similar values we shared. It could not have been more obvious that Greg was as sharp a business mind as they came and that he would be able to play an enormous role on the project—and hopefully on other projects in the future. As such, we agreed to be full partners—but there was still capital and financing to discuss.

"Do you have the capital lined up for this deal yet?" Greg asked.

"Well, yes, kind of," I said. "I'm working on it." The truth was that I didn't have the money—I had been putting out feelers, but it would take roughly $22 million to buy the debt (with immediate reserves of additional capital required for the next phases of development).

"My friend Charlie has some connections with Michael Dell and MSD Capital," Greg said. "But if we bring him in, he's going to become a partner as well." As it turned out, Greg had recently invited another slightly older guy named Charlie Phelan into his office to man a desk there temporarily. Charlie had just left one of the bigger real estate shops and had relationships with a lot of institutional investment firms. It sounded like a great opportunity, but before we could finalize it all, Greg, Charlie and I all had to meet to get on the same page. Sure enough, I hit it off with Charlie the same way I had with Greg, and we were soon ready to move forward.

In 2009, Miami condos were viewed as a toxic investment thesis. They were not a good look: all the cranes had stopped, and the whole market had gone up in flames, so locating investment funds had become very difficult. Investors were dealing with the fallout of the subprime mortgage crisis, so everyone was gun shy. Even so, Michael Dell had a multibillion-dollar fund that financed many different opportunistic investments, and this one seemed like a worthy opportunity to present.

Charlie and Greg reached out to Michael Dell's people to work on the financial side of things while I dealt with the bank from New York. Initially, MSD Capital said no. After a long conference call, we convinced them to fly someone down to Florida to check out our deal in person, but even after getting down there, they passed again. As a last-ditch effort, we convinced MSD to send someone *else* down to

Florida one last time to spend some time with us for a few more days.

The man they were planning to send down was Matt Olim, one of the higher-ups at the organization. I was scheduled to fly in from New York for the meeting, so I took the initiative of figuring out what flight he would be on and booked the same one. Before I'd gotten on the plane, I looked up his picture so I would recognize him on the plane. I got there as early as possible to board, and sure enough, I saw him sitting with an empty seat next to him—and I sat right down, even though my own real seat was 20 rows away.

"Are you Matt?" I asked.

He nodded, confused.

"I'm Daniel," I said. "I'm working with Charlie and Greg down in Miami. We're about to spend a few days together."

In the middle of my impromptu sales pitch, a woman walked up and interrupted me.

"Hey, yo, Papi," she said. "That's my seat." She had a tough energy about her, and I could tell from her accent that she was from the Bronx. Under any other circumstances, I would've just moved, but I knew there was no way I could get out of the seat. There were at least two-and-a-half hours of flight time ahead of us, and I planned to use all of it.

"Look, Miss," I told her firmly. "I apologize. I have to sit next to my friend. I really have to talk to him about something, and I'd be happy to pay for your seat. Anything I can do, I'll do; I just have to sit here." Matt was looking at me like I was out of my mind; meanwhile, the woman just rolled her eyes at me.

"Whatever," she said and stomped off to my seat in the back of the plane. Thankfully, the air stewards didn't make a big deal about it—and because we got stuck on the tarmac, my two-and-a-half hours turned into four. And during that time, I did as much as I could to warm Matt up to all the potential contained in our deal, despite the less-than-favorable conditions of the Florida real estate market. I hadn't even landed in Miami yet, but the persuasion process was already underway.

When we finally got to Miami, Charlie, Greg and I drove around with Matt in Charlie's old Honda Accord (in other words, a beat-up old shitbox). In Miami, everyone's usually showing off what they don't have; they might be driving a Maserati but living in a hovel. Charlie still saw the value in his car, so he kept it. Matt seemed to like that—it was clear we weren't flashy Miami guys.

Sure enough, after wining and dining Matt while explaining in detail why the deal would be so sweet, he finally agreed to take it upstairs at MSD. I flew back to New York, but all three of us agreed to get on a GoTo meeting for a video conference about the deal the following week (this was before the days of Zoom calls).

On the day of the call, the MSD guys were in Manhattan, I was in my office in New York and Greg and Charlie were in their Fort Lauderdale office. From the very beginning, the MSD guys were breaking down the structure and terms of the deal they were proposing, including what everybody would be taking home on the backend. To say they were offering us a very aggressive proposal would be an understatement; their terms were completely absurd. In fact, their first salvo was so offensive that by the time everything was factored in, Greg, Charlie and I would have basically been working for minimum wage. In the middle of the meeting, I started sending Greg a private message in all caps to vent a little bit:

WHAT THE FUCK ARE WE, BAGGAGE HANDLERS???

I could see from the screen share that I was getting a reaction from Greg, so I kept sending more messages:

We could be waiters at the Fontainebleau and make the same as what these guys are proposing.

I felt my phone buzz. It was Greg:

STOP MESSAGING.

What I didn't realize was I hadn't privately messaged Greg. Everyone on the conference call could see what I'd written on his screen (or so he thought). Since Greg was a little more tech-adept than I was, he disabled the chat window before I could do any more damage, and after MSD's first offer, we came back with our own. Finally, we landed on a deal that was marginally better than the first one and called it a day. There was no money on the street, so we had to take the best deal we could get. The most important thing was just to get a deal done—fortunately, the brand value of doing a deal with MSD Capital was a price above rubies.

With the details locked in place, all that was left was for Charlie, Greg and me to give the new company we were forming a name.

"So, what are we going to call this thing?" Greg asked with a smile; we all still couldn't believe what we had just been through.

"Well, I think it's only appropriate," I said. "We're going to be the three baggage handlers here, so let's call it that." We all laughed, and with that, BH3 was born.

When we went to finally close the deal in Manhattan, I brought along the TV spot about the Sherman Gardens flip to show Matt's boss Robert Platek and his special opportunities team. Robert was as seasoned as any real estate investor, so I figured he might need another boost of confidence in us to get him to sign. Right away, he was floored.

"Honestly," Robert said, "what you're showing me in this video was one of the reasons I wanted to do the deal with you. You're not going to sit around and take notes; you're going to get it done no matter what. No matter what's involved, how much you have to sweat, how much you have to live at the property. And those are the kind of people we want to invest with."

———

Because we approached the developers cooperatively, we were able to do more than just work with Sieger Suarez; we could also use their general contractor's license to push the project forward without having to pull new permits ourselves. It also meant we were avoiding two or three years of litigation, which would've sucked up endless time and energy. Even with those advantages, it was clear that this was going to be a bear of a deal.

There were many factors that made Terra Beachside so complex. For one thing, there were 120 mechanics' liens on the property, meaning tons of people that we would need to pay back or settle with for work they'd already completed. From the business side, construction was only about 65 percent complete, so we would have to finish it ourselves— but on top of that, most of the units were already in contract with buyers who were out of the money because the housing market had imploded. In other words, if someone had been under contract to buy one of the condos for $800,000 when they signed, in the interim period, their apartment was now only worth $400,000. Maybe that guy had put a deposit down to hold his place in line, but now he didn't want to close—after all, why throw good money after bad? It meant that we would have to wrestle those people and fight to keep their deposits, which we were legally entitled to for the most part—which was conceptually profitable but offered a low return on time. Once all that was done, we could get new buyers in for the units at a price we would set reflective of the current market.

We all agreed early on that to make the deal work, we couldn't have any ego involved. Whatever had to be done, we would do without complaint. In other words, it was unspoken that we would all lean aggressively into adversity. Above all, we would remember one thing: whatever road-blocks we ran into were the very reasons the property was such a huge opportunity in the first place.

The actual site was a beautiful, sleek compound of 13 buildings connected by catwalks, concrete platforms and glass railings. The property had an open atrium and Zen garden area that was covered by a big canopy that provided shade. All around the complex were Asian water features with bamboo shoots growing inside. They were gorgeous, but on our tight budget and while putting out so many fires, we had no money or time to hire a gardening or landscaping crew to take care of them. Very quickly, we remembered our newly minted mantra: keep ego out of it. With that thought reverberating through our minds, it became our job to water the shoots so we wouldn't have to dig them up and replace them when they died—and every partner picked up the hose.

At the same time, we had to adapt to the marketing side of the business very quickly as well. To do that, BH3 hired a handful of salesmen and set them up in an old, busted trailer on a neighboring site that we didn't even own. Because we were in a luxury market, the guys we hired were used to selling out of fancy offices and sales centers with all kinds of bells and whistles. Here, we put them in one of the sketchiest set-ups imaginable: trying to close new buyers for incomplete apartments with a deep bench of title issues (ranging from mechanics liens to contract vendee disputes) for prices that may have seemed exorbitant during a financial crisis that had frozen the Miami condo market, and all out of a busted trailer.

One rainy day, Greg and I were meeting with the sales team so they could air their grievances about the sales process. They explained they were having trouble selling because they needed a proper sales center, a driven car, fancy dinners and parties and so on when Charlie stuck his hand through the trailer window and cut them off: "You guys couldn't sell dick in a women's prison!" Greg and I cracked up; Charlie had ended the conversation.

When it came time to sell, the lawyers said we couldn't sell any units that were encumbered by pending foreclosure and countless mechanical liens. This was obviously a serious problem because, without the ability to sell units, we could not pay off our investment capital which was burning rapidly. We were determined to find a creative workaround. Greg and I met with our lawyers again and again to determine an angle, pressing for solutions where it seemed like there weren't any. It was clear that because the issues were happening at the level of the title, getting the title company to cooperate with us was crucial to seeing the project through to completion.

What we finally concluded was that as each unit sale transpired, and with the title company's cooperation, we would bond over a proportional share of the liens. In other words, if the entire project had $100,000 in liens, we would bond over $1/117^{th}$ of it for selling one of our 117 possible units—though we provided an additional 50 percent to ensure the units and allow the title company peace of mind in providing a clean title so we could move forward with the sales process. The reality was that once we washed the title through the foreclosure process, all the liens and encumbrances would be removed as well.

In spite of all the challenges, we managed to finish all the condos, resolve things with the contractors, mend the relationships with the existing buyers and fill the complex with new ones. Just as Robert at MSD had said at the very beginning, we weren't going to take no for an answer—and we were going to drive hard to see the project through to completion.

It had taken us about one year plus to turn it all around, but after changing the toxic narrative around the building and successfully putting it back out to market, we had made about $120 per square foot across 199,000 square feet of net sellable condominium product in profit. That was above our $154 per square foot cost basis, namely $84 per square foot to purchase the debt and another $70 to carry and complete it. In all, we had made $24 million and doubled our investment.

It was a perfect first experience for BH3—the deal had been hyper challenging in nearly every aspect, and yet we'd tackled it wholeheartedly and saw it through to the end. It showed us that there were no limits to the team we had put together, and our DNA was formed. Charlie, Greg and I hadn't done business together before, and we'd faced all kinds of situations that would test our mettle, our business ethics and our interactions with other people.

Deals with the pressure and scale that Terra Beachside had were special because they were able to magnify short durations of time into what seemed like years of experience. Even though Greg, Charlie and I had not known each other for very long, the depth and intensity of what we had endured together meant we had gotten to know each other very quickly, and we had bonded with lightning speed amidst the adversity. Coming through the other side of a deal that would've broken most partnerships, we felt as triumphant as an Ancient Roman triumvirate.

The deal exemplified our win-win philosophy that would go on to become our foundation. All of us wanted to ensure whenever possible that all the parties involved in a deal made out as best as possible, even under difficult circumstances. As a result of that shared mindset, we had pulled off an accomplishment even institutional investment firms would have to take notice of. It was the beginning of an ongoing joke we would repeat on virtually every project to come.

"This is it," Greg said to me with a shit-eating grin. "This is the deal that's going to put us on the map."

14

FULL CIRCLE ON TRUMP HOLLYWOOD

In the middle of our momentum on Terra Beachside, BH3 found another opportunity at the Fontainebleau. It was owned by Jeff Soffer of the Soffer family, a major real estate dynasty in Florida who were now in some financial trouble like so many other people were at that time. I did not see Jeff's situation as a failure; I only saw it as a badge of his boldness. He had taken a big swing, and as any prominent real estate developer or investor knows, market conditions could turn on anyone. He had built two condo towers, one of which, the ocean-facing Sorrento Tower, contained 25 apartments that were never sold and remained collateral to his hotel lender. The building was at 44th and Collins in Miami Beach, not far from where we were developing Terra Beachside, and it was an undeniably sexy opportunity. The deal was brought to us by a broker, and we locked it up.

It was a $10 million deal, and though we were rapidly getting better at fundraising, we were still relative novices at raising that amount of money. We scrambled as hard as we could to buy the entire block of units from Bank of America in a short sale with the help of $5 million in financing arranged by Eric Edidin and Archer Capital and some equity raise from Ari Goldman and his network. The deal itself was incredible, but it was also a veritable playground for Greg and me. In the process of selling those apartments, we would often work out of the area by the pool or the bar, holding court and setting meetings to find buyers. In less than a year, we had sold all of the units and made several million (though if we had held onto them, we would have made even more). It also opened the doors to doing more deals with Jeff Soffer, who had a large portfolio with his family, was very established in the area and had a lot of distressed debt from Florida to Vegas.

What BH3 had done together on Terra Beachside and the Fontainebleau had grown our name and reputation all around Miami. Although we had all grumbled a little about the harsh financial terms we agreed to with MSD Capital, what we lost in dollars we had more than made up for in marketing value and name recognition. Michael Dell and his company were not small names, and the fact that our modest firm had been able to partner with them said volumes about our character and abilities. Though we were still aggressively seeking out deals on our own, we were also taking a lot more phone calls in a very short period.

In 2009, I moved the family down to Florida to live in Delray Beach, ready to expand our footprint and reputation in the area even further. It was the same year Rachel and I had our second daughter, Tamir, who was born in Boca Raton Hospital. Just as we had experienced with Zoe, the experience was beautiful, life-affirming and full of celebration—though it was clear from day one that Tamir was entirely her own person. From the moment she came out of the womb, she was boisterous and had explosive energy. Although we could not control her but only hope to contain her, we could see a depth of thought and focus in her eyes that we knew would carry through her entire life.

"She's going to be a natural-born leader," I said to Rachel with a smile. As our family was growing alongside my business, I felt the fire in my gut to provide more than I ever had before—and I knew that the distressed real estate market in South Florida had more than enough opportunities to add fuel to it. I knew what the next deal would be: Trump Hollywood.

Right before the housing market had collapsed, Trump Hollywood had made its debut in Hollywood Beach. It was a $355 million project that hit the market right as all demand for luxury condominiums was disappearing, and now it was being foreclosed on. This was a huge opportunity. I was reminded of my one-time dream of buying a casino in Vegas before I had the experience to do so. This time, it looked like BH3 might have the seasoning and gumption to pull it off.

Trump Hollywood was a gorgeous 41-story building that was all glass and sat on five acres of premier beachfront property. All the condos came complete with the finest appliances—hell, it even had seven figures' worth of art just sitting in the lobby. The entire interior had been designed by Yabu Pushelberg, and the building itself was created by Robert Swedroe, a prestigious architect in South Florida. It was a magnificent oceanfront building beaming in the sunshine, a diamond in the rough. Still, it was 2010—even if there were plenty of big players in line to scoop up the property at a massive discount, everyone was telling us to stay the hell away from it. We heard every line in the book:

"The way that deal is structured is a disaster. There's no way you don't lose money on it."

"Even if you get control, the units are way too big, and you'll never be able to fill them."

"There's no buyers out there—you're biting off more than you can chew!"

Without a doubt, the entire business world was still at a relative standstill, and the economy hadn't rebounded. Even so, getting a chance to buy something this pristine (albeit by way of its non-performing loan) at such a massive markdown rarely if ever happened. We knew we had to figure out who owned the banknote first and after a little digging, we found out it was HSBC Bank. To find an in, we started thinking strategically about our networks.

"Who do we know at their law firm?" Greg asked. "Or who do we know at HSBC Bank?"

We were all working our own angles, but after looking through my contacts, I couldn't believe it—I did know someone who was a higher-up at HSBC Bank! Mike Wadler, who had mentored me in my days of working at the Maidmans, had ended up there. As soon as I realized that, I reached out to him to strike up a conversation—and before long, their bank was hyper-focused on BH3 as a potential partner to relaunch Trump Hollywood.

After working the bank for several months, we had lined up a preliminary deal to purchase the note on the building for $164 million, but we had very little time to close. To make things even more nebulous, we didn't even have a contract—just a gentleman's agreement that if we could put it together, HSBC would go with us. On the strength of that, we started hunting for capital as fast as we could. Just like with the Terra Beachside deal, Charlie said he had a connection at an investment firm that we might be able to bring in.

After a good first meeting, BH3's lawyers and the firm's lawyers started duking it out over contract specifics, but all seemed to be going well. It looked like they were on board and ready to fund us—that is until they heard that we had no contract with HSBC Bank.

"Listen, Daniel," one of their lead deal guys told me over the phone, "we're not going to invest half a million in legal fees on a deal that we don't even know we have."

"I understand where you're coming from," I replied, "but you've got to have a little faith here. These bankers are absolutely committed to us. It goes beyond business! We know they will trade to us if we stick to the timeline and continue down the path with conviction" It wasn't enough to move them.

"It's too much risk," the guy replied. "We can't burn half a million dollars without a contract, Daniel. I'm sorry I have to say it."

The news couldn't have come at a worse time. We'd been carefully researching and building the deal, and now, with a week left to close, our capital partners were pulling out. Still, I wasn't about to give up—finding a replacement capital partner for a deal this massive in a week was a nearly impossible task, but the keyword there was *nearly*. The opportunity was too good, and we had to try.

"I understand your position, and I won't push you," I said. "But listen—please stick around or at least appear to stick around for the time being. We don't have much time left, but we'd like to try and find a replacement partner, and I don't want the bank to get scared by seeing that you guys weren't interested."

Sure enough, they said they could do that for us as a courtesy, and the phone call was over; it was a testament to the rapport and relationship we had built with them. Afterward, I had to debrief with Greg on what we were about to try to do.

"I think this is the big one, Daniel," he said. "I know I've said it before, but—this is the one that's going to put us on the map." What could I do but laugh?

Right away, Greg, Charlie and I scrambled like never before to find someone who might want in on the deal. It was a true do-or-die situation. Finally, we found a potential replacement in King Street Capital, a major institution that could turn our entire situation around. We got on the phone with them and convinced them to fly someone down immediately to look at the property with us. That call was on Tuesday night, and right after, they had a flight booked to come down to Florida on Wednesday, the next day.

On Wednesday, we were all touring the property together, and it was clear that they were impressed with the specs of the deal and the due diligence we'd already done. After discussing the particulars for a few more days (and with more and more time on the clock winding down), touring comparable buildings, it was time to escalate the deal to the higher-ups. Friday came, and their head lawyer Chris reached out to us.

"Everything looks good on this so far, but we need to speak to the current owners of the property," Chris said. "We need to talk to the developers so we can understand how challenging the litigation will be." Fuck. From our perspective, we wanted control regardless of the litigation. As the debtholders, we were ready to fight no matter what, but we knew most institutions would not feel similarly.

Even if what they were saying made sense, a foreclosure on a property of that size is not a kind, cozy interaction between cooperative parties. It's often an overtly hostile takeover. Asking to talk to the developers was like going across enemy lines. To make it worse, the developer was Jorge Perez, known as "the Condo King" in South Florida. The guy was a multi-billionaire who commanded the real estate market in the area, and he likely had the busiest schedule imaginable—there wasn't even a guarantee he was in the country that week, let alone the state. On top of all that, there was no doubt in my mind that he had an entire panel of high-powered lawyers at his disposal who would tell us to go fuck ourselves and poison the waters in any way they could. But I didn't say any of that.

"I understand," I told Chris. "We'll arrange that meeting, and I'll reach out soon with the details." After hanging up, I started looking through my contacts yet again. I knew I would need some serious assistance if we were going to get a meeting with Jorge Perez over the weekend for a deal we needed to close by 5 pm that coming Tuesday (just before the mezzanine foreclosure auction took place).

I reached out to Jimmy Tate, who was the president of Tate Capital. I had met him in 2009 while trying to buy a deal off him that he had locked from Regions Bank—the same bank from which we bought the debt on Terra Beachside. From our first bagel breakfast, I could tell Jimmy was an old-school businessman in the truest sense, which endeared him to me immediately. As it turned out, Jimmy's dad had worked for the Carter administration and was a well-established real estate guy in South Florida in his own right. Though we'd taken some meetings, we'd never done business together before because we had never lined up anything that had worked for both of us. Even so, we had a good rapport, and he knew Jorge well enough to get me a phone call with some of the senior guys at his company, the Related Group. We broke the news to them about our plans for the property and explained that our capital partners wanted to speak with them about terms.

What happened next was exactly what I thought was going to happen.

"You think we're just going to give you the keys here?" Matt Allen, Related Group's chief operating officer, said in total disbelief. They were barely stifling their laughter. "There's no way in hell," Matt said. We're going to fight you tooth and nail on this, and you're going to wish you never got involved. We're going to drag this out. Even if you make it through all the litigation that's coming, we'll make sure you don't sell a condo on this project for five years."

Even though I knew they were coming, I could not have written words I wanted to hear less than those—and because it was a conference call, the lawyer at King Street Capital, Chris, had heard it all as well.

After that call ended, the next one I got was from him.

"Daniel, are you fucking insane?" Chris shouted into the phone. "You think we're going to invest with you on this? This deal isn't firmed up at all! This is completely unstable! There's no way we can give you money. Jesus, I'm going to lose my job over this!"

"Chris, please," I said as calmly as I could under the circumstances. "You have to trust us. Did you think they were going to say they would leave the building keys in the lobby for us? We still have time, so all you have to do is keep the lawyers and the entire team working. Let your guys do what they do best, and let us do what we do best. We will get you the deed before closing."

"How the hell are you going to do that?" he asked. To be honest, I was thinking the same thing.

"Please just trust me," I said simply. "I will get you the deed before closing; you just have to let me handle it."

After the phone call ended, I called Jimmy again. I needed another meeting with Jorge or his team, and it had to be in person this time.

After some back and forth with King Street, they had authorized BH3 to spend one million of their money up front if it meant we could secure the deed so the deal could continue. Meanwhile, both our partners and we were spending tens of thousands of dollars to keep a stable of lawyers and analytics staff working throughout negotiations and deep diligence, all of which seemed destined to fail. All the same, Jimmy lined up a meeting where BH3 would meet with Jorge on Sunday night—with just 48 hours left to get the deed, secure financing and wire the money to HSBC.

We were very careful approaching that meeting. We knew we had the authority to spend some money, but we also knew that Related was completely out of the money on their property. They could fight us out of ego and spite, but there was really no upside for them. They were deeply underwater, and they knew it. With that in mind, I knew there might be a way to turn the deal around. As it turned out, it wasn't Jorge who turned up to the meeting, but two of his lead guys, Matt Allen and another guy. It felt like an unexpected advantage. After negotiating, we made them an offer for $500,000 with some tail-end deal kickers to make things interesting.

"To make things as fair as we can here," I said, "we're willing to give you some points on the backend out of our end. Right now, this is a toxic asset for you, but if we make this deal, it doesn't have to be. We will finish it, and it'll be cash-producing again. So do we have a deal?" Finally, they agreed.

After that, we took the elevator downstairs to the lobby of Related's office building where I called Chris on the phone.

"How did it go?" he asked impatiently.

"They're ready to sign," I said. "Let's get them the papers immediately."

"They're ready to sign? You gave them a million dollars?"

"No, I gave them half a million, and they're going to come in on the sales side with us," I replied. "It's all good; just get them the papers." I could almost hear his jaw coming unhinged on the other end.

A large team of lawyers was working to finalize not only the purchase of the loan, the deed in lieu, but also our joint venture documents with both King Street and Related. One of the reasons Perez and his team were amenable to inking a deal was because they knew the best thing was to clear up toxicity quickly to focus on the future of their well-crafted business. It was a testament to their experience and wisdom, as many borrowers would never do that; many would choose to fight instead, even if it came at great personal expense, loss of mass swaths of time, and outright distraction from building anew. In our case, the timing was another dollop of good fortune tethered to our savvy.

After everything, we collected all the signatures we needed by late afternoon on Tuesday, most importantly the deed in lieu and Related Companies releases. We handed over the final papers to King Street Capital, and they sent a wire of $164 million for the first mortgage and mezzanine position into HSBC's accounts at 4:32 pm that day—28 minutes before the deadline. Even we couldn't believe it: somehow, we'd pulled it off in six and a half days. We had successfully purchased the note on Trump Hollywood, and we'd done it without pouring salt in anyone's wounds. Instead, we'd found a new potential future partnership with Related and Jorge Perez under some of the highest stakes imaginable (I later found out that had we failed to close the deal then and there, a backup buyer was sitting at HSBC headquarters to hit the wire).

The next big decision to make was what to do about the branding. Because it was called Trump Hollywood, it was associated with their name and their brand; if our plan was to completely make it our own, we would have to take their name off the building and renegotiate with them. Even though this was before the 2016 presidential election, it was still a situation with many sensitivities.

To begin the process, we met with the Trump family and their organization to determine the next steps. After talking it all through, we decided to target not only American and Canadian buyers but also buyers in Latin America. The clincher was that in Latin America, the Trump brand was extraordinarily popular. It was thought of as a very high-end brand, and it only made sense to play into it. The final decision was that we would keep the name.

Because the deal had been so difficult up to that point, we were so relieved that the family was so cooperative. At the launch party, I had to take a moment to speak to Donald Trump.

"Excuse me, Mr. Trump," I said, extending my hand for a shake. "I'm not sure if you remember me, but I chased you down once on the steps of court in New York City asking for a job. I just want to thank you for not hiring me—not getting that job changed my entire life."

After the negotiations ended, we inked a license renewal with the Trump family, and we went to work on packaging and selling our units. We hired a sales team and put plans in place for advertising, social media strategy, public relations and broker meetings. Within 18 months, we sold the place out for approximately $276 million and made a highly successful exit. Everyone had told us we were going to get our asses handed to us, but the opposite had proven true. At the very end of the project, Donald even put out a congratulatory video online in his signature effusive style:

"Those BH3 guys are fantastic," he said. "There are a lot of nice buildings out there, but they got it done here. Those other guys don't sell as well as you guys do!"

15

RENOVATIONS WITH A RABBI

As BH3 grew, distressed debt deals continued to fuel our ascent and offered us some of the funniest stories. On one deal, one of our more religious partners went behind our backs to forgive a borrower's defaulted debt—so long as he agreed to get circumcised. There was another note on Rivington Street with a difficult borrower called Ben Z with whom I had tried to reason, but to no avail. In typical fashion, when one of us could not get a deal done, we handed the gavel over to the other without ego or hesitation—just with the mission in mind.

As such, Greg tried his hand at the negotiations with Ben and was told instead to roll the mortgage up and shove it into his wife's sacred of sacreds. You might think this would have infuriated Greg, but he found it was so preposterous that it was hilarious. With the greatest respect to Greg's wife, Mara, who has been a great sport about such an absurd and inappropriate comment, Greg and I still crack up about that to this day. Through dozens and dozens of these situations, our company was growing, and we were learning that was no end to the dramatics one could find themselves in when it came to investing in distressed debt.

After the two huge wins of Terra Beachside and Trump Hollywood, BH3 was making a real name for itself in Florida —and we were using that momentum to take on more and more distressed assets. By 2012, we had a playbook and a structure we followed in one way or another on almost every deal.

Generally, we first bought the note from the bank and then foreclosed through to the asset level. After taking over the asset somehow (using a cooperative or collaborative approach whenever possible), we would renovate it on the ground level if necessary, rebrand and repackage it with the help of marketing and sales experts and finally put it back out to market. We were starting to build our expertise in buying non-performing loans and using our respective legal and financial backgrounds to restructure, prosecute foreclosures, get creative with financing, bring in partners and figure out the marketing and branding after all that.

Though we were always looking wherever we could for new value, we had found a system that worked and mostly wanted to stay in our lane. Of course, those are always the times when life throws you a curveball.

BH3 had moved offices into Trump Hollywood when a local investor brought us a potential new deal.

"I've got a great opportunity here to buy the debt on this property at 4000 Alton Road," he said. "It used to be a Howard Johnson's, but now it's Rohr Talmudic University, this religious non-profit. They're being foreclosed on. This could be a really great development site."

Rohr Talmudic University was a yeshiva not unlike the one I'd gone to as a kid—basically a Jewish learning institute for religious kids run by rabbis. Now, this man was saying that as this religious cultural center was about to lose everything, we could tear down everything they'd built and do it over again to make a profit? I was willing to make money in many different circumstances, but this wasn't one of them.

"What is this?" I said, my voice rising a little. "Why would you think we'd be interested in this? This rabbi is getting crushed, and you want us to step on him even harder? Forget it—life's too short, and there are plenty of other deals to do without worrying about the karma and headaches of foreclosing a religious institution."

After chewing him out a little, I sent him on his way— and to their credit, Charlie and Greg wanted nothing to do with it either. Though we thought we'd put it to bed, he reached out again later about the same property, this time more insistently.

"I know you said you didn't want to be involved in foreclosing on a religious institution," he said, "but you really need to take a look at this. You need to see what's going on, and maybe you guys can work something out." We could tell we weren't going to get away from this one, so we agreed to meet with the rabbi.

As it turned out, Rabbi Yitzy Zweig was a lovely guy who was very well-known and liked around Miami—as were all his children, who were also rabbis. He showed us the property, and we spoke for a while. After getting the lay of the land, I could see why the deal was so tempting; the geography and the location were perfect. Early on, he invited us to a Shabbat dinner so that all three of us could break bread and discuss the coming months. As he explained his reasoning behind buying the Howard Johnson years earlier to renovate for his own religious uses, I could sense that he had a very keen business mind.

"It seemed like a great opportunity to hold a space for our community here in Miami," Rabbi Yitzy said. "Our presence here lets us do more outreach, help more of the poor members of our community, particularly the younger ones. My dream was for this to continue to be a home base and a place for the youth to learn about the Jewish faith." His face fell a little at this, not knowing our plans for the property. "Daniel, do you have a family?"

Our conversation quickly turned from a business discussion to a heart-to-heart about life, faith and family—as well as the benefits of giving back, our mutual support of Israel and of doing charitable work. It was unclear what would happen next, but we established a non-adversarial relationship from the beginning.

"Regardless of what you would like to do here," Rabbi Yitzy said, "please come to the bank with me. I'm not telling you and your team to do anything; just please come talk to the bank by my side." We were unsure of the path forward, but he'd been nothing but kind and polite in our interactions, so we agreed to come with him.

The day came when Charlie, Greg and I all met Rabbi Yitzy at a prominent national bank—and as he had promised, it was a thoroughly unpleasant meeting. A level of unnecessary roughness was clearly at play. Rabbi Yitzy wasn't trying to pull one over on the bank or game the system—he had just run out of money and needed a little bit of mercy. He was running a non-profit during hard times, and charitable donations had dried up—donations that those kinds of institutions relied on. He had taken out another mortgage with plans to develop more rooms and dormitories on his property, but it hadn't worked out, and now he was even deeper underwater. I could understand his position. He was a private entrepreneur just like I had been. And he was in the religious world rather than the secular.

Because we were there mostly to observe, we stayed out of Rabbi Yitzy's way and let him do the talking and negotiating—but all three of us walked out with a very sour impression. It was my Irish and thoroughly non-Jewish partner Charlie (although he is rumored to love Klezmer music) who said what we were all thinking.

"Those guys are filled with hate," he spat. "I've never seen anything like that before. They're anti-Semites, for sure!" All three of us agreed. It was clear we had to jump in and do justice here, but it was unclear what exactly—though all three of us were generating the best ideas we could.

"There's no way we can leave him to suffer at the hands of these guys," I said. "I know this is out of our zone, but maybe we can figure something out here."

As soon as we started looking into the deal and the property more closely, it turned out that Rabbi Yitzy only needed the north part of his site to keep doing what he'd been doing. The south side was mostly an oversized parking lot, but it had potential as a development site. It wasn't very big, so it wouldn't offer much square footage, but it was definitely worth looking into—particularly if it meant helping someone in need while doing something for ourselves as well.

The first thing we did was try to frame out a deal with the bank to buy the debt. They set the price at $5.4 million, and while we tried to negotiate down, they wouldn't discount it at all. The next issue was raising the money to buy the debt, which we primarily obtained from Harry Zubli's family—namely his uncle Isaac and his cousin Ari. Harry's family was religious, and they appreciated what we were taking on by protecting the yeshiva. With enough money raised, the full pricing didn't matter—there was no way we were going to let the bank win. Afterward, we came back to announce the next steps to everyone at the yeshiva.

"Rabbis, the good news is that we're not going to foreclose on your property," I said to them as they breathed a huge sigh of relief. "That's number one. Number two is that we're going to collaborate here to turn this project into something we can all benefit from."

Between us and legal, we engineered a reframing of the deal that was more beneficial to everyone involved. After explaining our plan to them and getting their approval, we decided to go to the city and get the south side of the property rezoned. We decided to do a covenant in lieu of unity of title to keep the plots together while also allowing for some separation. It meant the two lots could share some common elements like the parking lot and the driveway while remaining legally distinct—the shared elements were just so both properties were both functional from an infrastructural perspective.

The entire time we were putting the deal together, Greg, Charlie and I were investigating the property as thoroughly as we could and looking for other angles to add density to the development site. One of the things that stood out was on the map, there was a road that came across the bay that split into a V, and our property sat right in the middle of it. Around that V-shaped area was some storm drainage abutting the two roads, all of which was owned by the Department of Transportation.

Again, it sounded like an opportunity. Even though it was just a few disconnected slivers of land here and there, when you added them all up, you added square footage to develop on because, in theory, you could capture their density allowance—and it didn't seem impossible that the DOT could be talked into parting with it. From the very beginning, we knew what dealing with the government could be like—we would likely get caught in bureaucracy and may never get an answer. Even so, it was worth a shot.

As we were putting everything together, dealing with the city and thinking about our development plans, we were gradually accumulating slivers of land until we qualified for a development that would support 65,000 square feet of condominiums. Because we had that much footage, we could also apply for air rights that would let us build 81 feet up instead of 60, which would give the place great views of the water—another huge value add. When it came time for us to build, we were getting the sense that the market was too frothy, and we didn't like the timing. We had already entitled the property, so we had the optionality to develop it or sell it as-is for an extraordinary profit and walk away clean and clear. Finally, we agreed to sell the south side of the site to another company for $18.2 million.

When all was done, we scheduled a final Shabbat dinner with Rabbi Yitzy. He introduced us to his father, who was the head of the yeshiva and who thanked us for all we had done.

"We have more good news for you," I said. "Our collaboration has been so successful that we are going to dissolve your obligations to us. We're forgiving the $5.4 million mortgage on your portion of the property so you can walk away free and clear." Rabbi Yitzy and his father were in disbelief and tried to resist (in the same way people fight over a restaurant bill since we all knew what was ultimately going to happen), but Greg and I insisted—we had done well financially by working with them, but receiving the rabbi's wisdom and warmth over the course of many heart-to-hearts was not something you could put a price on. We had made a new lifelong friend.

"Thank you," Rabbi Yitzy said. "This is an incredible mitzvah you've done for us here." On top of forgiving his debt, BH3 also donated money to him to help him redesign with his architect and build a bigger version of what he had there already. The beautiful thing was that the initial $5.4 million to buy the note wasn't even money we put in ourselves; we had taken out leverage for most of it.

As a company, we each put in around $120,000 apiece up front. Along the way, it cost us another $2 million to buy the government land and pay the lawyers to hash out the details, bringing our initial investment up to $7.4 million. In all, it meant that we had walked away with $9 million in profit in just under two years. In the process, we had saved a religious institution, protected a good man with a great family and freed him up to focus on strengthening the community. We had made a profit, but all the other benefits were so much greater.

Though getting involved with a yeshiva foreclosure had sounded like a nightmare initially, it was a grounding exercise in more ways than one. I was reminded of my spiritual roots as well as my entrepreneurial roots of finding ways to squeeze value in ways other people didn't see. It was also a testament to BH3's partnership that we had all agreed to do the deal the right way and for the right reasons—and still make a huge profit on it. After multiple deals together, the BH3 team was growing, our processes were improving and it felt like there was nothing we couldn't take on.

It was a good place to be because we were about to walk into the biggest fight of our lives.

16

PRIVÉ AND A BRIEF HISTORY OF SOUTH FLORIDA REAL ESTATE

Back in 1975, Norman Cohen was a true pioneer. He bought more than 1,000 acres of land in South Florida, around 200 of which were in what is now Aventura, Florida. As much of the land was submerged, he dredged it, filled it and reworked it through development and title work until it became a massive plot zoned for more than 7,000 units. It was a developer's dream, and he began breaking the plot up into tracts and selling them off for a handsome profit.

Over time, the plot was broken up for many different uses including 15 high-rises near Aventura, mid-rises, dozens of townhomes, commercial offices, shopping centers and plenty of infrastructure. Along the way, he picked up two islands in a foreclosure sale during the oil crisis in the 1970s, which were right in the middle of Dumfoundling Bay in North Miami. The Cohen family held onto the islands through a family trust for some 40 years and left one of them undeveloped. The final island was to be the crown jewel in an already illustrious real estate portfolio that the Cohen family had put together, a kind of "final chapter" to a long real estate legacy. We didn't enter their story until 2012.

For me, it started when I got a call from Greg on a Wednesday telling me about a new opportunity for BH3.

"I just got a call from Steven G," he said. Steven was a renowned interior designer and a great businessman who had worked with us on Terra Beachside and had long been an angel on our shoulders. "He was telling me that we have to set up a meeting with Gary Cohen." As he explained, Gary owned an island in the bay near Miami that was undeveloped, a project we could really sink our teeth into. Initially, just that statement alone made no sense—an undeveloped island in Miami? In 2012? Greg gave me some basic details and told me I had to meet Gary. It sounded interesting, but I didn't think much of it. A day later, I got another call from my condo attorney, Howard Vogel.

"Daniel, I just spoke to my client, Gary Cohen," Howard said. Immediately, my ears perked up.

"Gary Cohen? Greg just called me yesterday to arrange a meeting with him," I said.

"He has a very interesting opportunity for BH3," Howard said. "He's a wonderful guy but he needs a company like yours—a company that won't try to steamroll him on this, people who will work together with him to do something really special." Hearing about the same guy twice in two days was enough to get me interested, so Greg, Charlie and I set up a meeting with Gary.

Sitting down with him, we learned the entire history of the Cohen family in Aventura and how his father Norman had laid the groundwork for so much later development. We learned how his father had acquired the islands and how it had taken so long to find the right partner and work around red tape to develop the last one.

"What I'm looking for on this project is to do something beautiful," Gary said. "It's the last significant piece of undeveloped land our family owns, and I don't want it to be just like everything else. I don't want another high-density highrise like the ones on Williams Island. I want something more elegant."

In a first meeting, all the parties are sizing each other up; just as we were vetting Gary, Gary was vetting us as well. As it turned out, part of his vetting process was calling his architects, who had worked with him on the last iteration of the project. What we didn't know, however, was that his architects were none other than Sieger Suarez, who had only the best things to say about us! Later, we called them all together and marveled at the reputational ripple effects that we had generated.

Right away, Greg and I knew that we'd walked into something special. Gary was more than a decade older than me, but he came across as humble and displayed an uncommon level of taste. If he was going to develop these islands, it would be a star addition to a long and prolific family real estate portfolio, so it had to be more than just a building. It had to be a work of art. With what we'd heard, we were ready to go to work putting a deal together.

After a few more meetings, Greg, Charlie and I came back to Gary with a proposal. In discussion among the BH3 partners was the possibility of developing a full-density highrise, as having more units to sell or rent could mean greater returns in good market conditions (and for that reason, it tended to be the primary modus operandi for many developers in Aventura). Still, Gary had a different perspective. On the one hand, yes, higher density could correlate with greater returns in good conditions, but the inverse could be true as well. Developing a luxury project at the scale we were considering was a tightrope walk in so many ways, and all of us had seen firsthand in Florida what sub-optimal market conditions could do to otherwise promising developments.

For his part, Gary proposed that we build a high-rise of moderate height with a lower unit count but with units that were considerably more spacious. The more we discussed, the clearer it was how this lateral thinking would fit with BH3's penchant for breaking convention and developing special projects. Each unit would be a "home in the sky" that averaged 3,400 square feet. Overall, the density would be similar, but the building height would be reduced while unlocking more than 70,000 square feet of common areas and amenities, making the entire complex more elegant and opening it up for design details and interior decoration. In the end, those areas would be like a museum with volumes of art from around the world. It would be an even more luxurious end product than Aventura was used to, and it was a vision we could all agree on.

After some debate, we agreed to pay Gary's robust price tag and to honor his intention not to build at full-density because we were aligned in finding ways to get the value back through our mutual creativity and by standing out. Though that part of the deal wasn't a huge issue, there were other creative differences to work through from the beginning.

"We're happy not to build high-density here, but we

have to collaborate in reconceiving your project," I told Gary. In his initial vision, Gary saw the island as a perfect place to build something great and had originally intended to create luxury, Mediterranean-style villas there—but as the market turned, and knowing what was selling and what wasn't, we all agreed that we needed to pivot in the redesign. What people in Miami wanted now were sleek and modern condominiums made with sheets of glass and concrete.

Within two weeks, we signed a term sheet with him to buy the property and started to negotiate the balance. The deal came with a $60 million sale price on the land, half of which Gary and his family put into the deal as development equity. We were responsible for finding the other $30 million.

We reached out into our network and got in touch with Isaac and Ari Zubli once more. Like they had done on the yeshiva deal, they showed incredible moxie and put millions in the deal—some in equity, some as a loan—at a time when it was incredibly risky to do so. I had developed a very strong stomach for risk and distress over the years, but what they were doing was extraordinary even to me; if the tables were turned, I wasn't sure I would have the balls to put up so much money.

"You boys will do well here," Isaac said as calmly as you please. "We know you'll do well by us if you stay focused. You can run like wild horses as far as I'm concerned, we trust you." It was music to any developer's ears, and their confidence only gave me more strength to get in a pugilist's mindset—just like I'd had as a young man on Long Island, only now with more purpose and exponentially superior returns. In all, we raised $48 million, an additional $18 million plus the $30 million contribution from Gary's family.

From the outset of the deal, we couldn't have been happier. BH3 was coming off a string of personal and professional successes and our name was becoming known in South Florida. Having a chance to develop an island in Aventura with a local real estate titan with such a high taste level was amazing—and there were seemingly few obstacles in our path. Unfortunately, that feeling was short-lived.

After we signed with Gary, we all met with the city of Aventura and verified our paperwork and rights to develop. Based on the island entitlements, namely Gary's vested rights, we were able to proceed with the beginnings of construction under administrative site plan review. Soon after, word got around in the neighborhood and it was not well-received. It was a controversy decades in the making.

The reason Gary's island had gone undeveloped for so long was not solely that he hadn't found the right partner. Part of the issue was the infrastructure-related issues and red tape around building bridges to the island so people could get in and out—and it was complicated by many factors. One of them dated all the way back to how Gary's father Norman had framed out the entitlements on what was now Williams Island in the 1970s.

In the 1970s, the Williams Tract (as it was then called) was owned by Norman Cohen, who was looking to sell it. Norman owned many more acres in the surrounding area, but because the Florida real estate market had taken a swing, he had come down from New York to protect his investment. It meant selling the Williams Tract under duress to Jules Trump, a South African businessman (of no relation to

Donald Trump) who had started developing real estate in South Florida.

While Gary's father Norman was developing the southern part of what is now Aventura, the Soffers were developing the northern end—and what they were doing there was capturing Jules's attention. When Jules and Norman made their original deal in 1979, Jules's original concept was to have a private road that allowed access to both islands. In the agreement, it was stated that there would be a dedicated road offering unimpeded access to both islands—but as Jules developed Williams Island, he changed his mind.

In the late 1970s and early 1980s, the Soffer family saw the opportunity to push luxury real estate development in the Miami area further than it had ever gone before. With money pouring into the area from Mexico, Soffer raised the bar for real estate prices in the area and was selling out at $100 a foot—an absolutely unheard-of price at the time. Jules fell in love with that idea of luxury and exclusivity, but he wanted to do it at $200 a foot.

To justify the higher prices, Jules's purchasers wanted him to close off access to Williams Island to make the community even more exclusive. To do so, they wanted gate-houses and security staff for each of 13 different buildings. He soon realized it would be easier to just build one security booth at the mouth of the island, cutting off unwanted visitors at the pass. Still, doing so would violate his agreement with Norman.

To settle things, Jules met with Norman and asked if he could build one guardhouse at the front of the island rather than many separate ones, despite what they'd initially agreed upon. After negotiation, Norman gave permission for the guardhouse to stand for four years, at which point Jules would have to take it down and make whatever other adjustments he needed to make to keep the Williams Island residents happy. Though they'd made the agreement, after more than four years (and some additional negotiations) had passed, Jules didn't want to take it down—and the two developers ended up in court.

In 1990, a judge made the decision to split the difference between Norman and Jules's wishes. He told Williams Island that they didn't have to take the guardhouse down entirely; instead, they could convert the two lanes on the road that passed through it. One of the lanes would remain open to allow the "unimpeded access" that was originally agreed upon and the other one could be closed or private.

After all those years had passed, Gary still had vested rights to develop his island as he saw fit, all underpinned by the agreement that Norman had framed out decades before. It meant that we could build a major development at Privé and Williams Island wouldn't be able to restrict access. Future Privé residents would have to be allowed to drive in and out of Williams Island freely every day, despite their attempts to make it a private community. Clearly, the idea of additional traffic and disrupting that uneasy local balance of power didn't sit well with Williams Island.

Around 30 or 45 days after we'd signed our initial deal with Gary, Williams Island hit us with a lawsuit: a declaratory action challenging our right to build. After it was announced, Gary called a meeting with Greg, Charlie and me.

"Look, you guys seem like really good guys," Gary said.

"I really wasn't expecting this lawsuit and I think it's nonsense, but I also bet we settle in 30 days. I don't want you to get sucked into this, so I'm happy to tear up the documents we signed right now. Once I have it cleared up, we can do this deal."

It was a testament to Gary's character to give us an out, but it never crossed our mind to leave. We didn't even have to confer privately on that point.

"Gary, you don't know who you partnered with," I replied. "We're not going anywhere. We love a good fight, and the rights are clearly yours. We're going to get this done together." He was pleasantly surprised, and we decided to push forward as planned, albeit with greatly increased risk. The new development was going to be called Privé at Island Estates—we had all come up with names and voted, but Greg's won the day.

17

THE NEVER-ENDING LAWSUIT

"The best thing in life is to go ahead with all your plans and your dreams, to embrace life and to live every day with passion, to lose and still keep the faith, and to win while being grateful. All of this because the world belongs to those who dare to go after what they want. And because life is really too short to be insignificant."
    -Charlie Chaplin

Even without facing a legal battle, Privé was a massive undertaking from the very beginning. It wasn't a busted project that we had come in to finish—instead, it was a project that would cost $365 million, including the hard costs of actually building the complex and the soft costs of marketing, architectural fees, civil engineering and so on. In concrete terms, our task was to construct luxury condominiums on an island surrounded by private and government property while fighting off a frivolous multimillion-dollar lawsuit and a peninsula full of angry property owners. All the while, we were assembling a robust legal team to defend ourselves in litigation.

Because BH3 was a boutique company and Privé was an enormous project, we had to work every local angle imaginable to make things make sense financially. In Florida, even with a construction loan, you don't need the entire balance of the equity to start developing a major project. Florida borrows some of its construction finance guidelines from Latin America and lets developers put up to 90 percent of buyers' deposits on apartments into the hard costs of building the actual apartments themselves. It was just another reason to hit the ground running with sales.

Through our sales team's hard work, we had sold our development out to about 50 percent capacity and were ready to move the center and start building. Meanwhile, the litigation against us was heating up. Before we were set to appear in court in front of a judge and representatives from the city of Aventura, Gary walked Greg and me through why we had nothing to worry about again and again.

"The vested rights my family negotiated years ago are very clear here," Gary assured us. "We've been upfront with the city. All they have to do is affirm that we're correct and that we're in good standing with them. On their word, the judge will have to rule in our favor, and this suit should be over in six months."

It sounded like things would go our way, but when we were all standing in front of the judge, Aventura's representatives surprised us. They confirmed that we'd spoken to them, acted in good faith and gotten their approval. Then they threw us a curveball.

"Your honor," the city representative said, "though we previously gave our approval, we'd like to see this matter resolved to the satisfaction of all parties involved. For that reason, it's our recommendation that this court use its own judgment in evaluating the basis of the developers' claims."

We couldn't believe what we were hearing. Because we'd met with the city of Aventura to go over our rights to build, and they'd given us the go-ahead, we assumed they would do the right thing in court by repeating what they had told us to the judge—namely, that we were in the right. Unfortunately, the Williams Island suit had changed their incentives. As a voting bloc in Aventura, Williams Island was highly influential. Keeping them on the city's side was important to them for many reasons, so it seemed to be to their advantage not to take a side. Instead, they could punt and let the court figure things out. The result of that one action was that the judge denied a summary judgment. At that point, we had no choice but to counter sue the city of Aventura for not standing by their word.

It was becoming clear that we were going to be in and out of court throughout the entire project—and it was also becoming clear to the buyers we'd already signed. Initially, we had sold 50 percent of our yet-to-be-constructed condos on the promise that the location would be beautiful and elegant and that the litigation would be over quickly. Now that it was clear it wouldn't be, buyers began pulling out until we were down to only 20 or 30 percent sold. On other projects, that kind of drawdown might have been enough to scrap a project altogether. But this wasn't just any project.

Considering the new obstacles we faced, we called Gary again to discuss our options. The joint venture we had with Gary was paying a substantial amount of money to keep the lawyers working and defend ourselves, and our potential losses on the project were seemingly uncapped. From BH3's end, we weren't a large firm with endless amounts of money laying around. We were putting everything we had into the project, and it had the potential to take down the entire company if things didn't go our way. Fortunately, we all had the same basic idea: we would fight to the death to prove we were right.

Though it was unclear how the litigation would go, the discussion we had was what would happen if we didn't win our lawsuit. In theory, if the judge ruled in favor of Williams Island, we would owe a lot of money and might be ordered to tear down anything we'd already built. Still, the more we thought about it, the more unlikely it seemed that a judge would actually force us to do that.

"Lawsuit aside, this is a race against time," Gary said. "We have a path to permits to start building, so we have to push ahead as aggressively as we can. The more of our project we've already legally built, the harder it will be for anyone else to order us to tear it all down."

This strategy meant that we would be pushing ahead at even greater financial and personal risk, but we couldn't deny that it made sense.

"The biggest obstacle, however," Gary said, "is the sidewalk." It was true.

Williams Island was southwest of Privé and South Island, which was populated by townhouses and jutted off into Dumfoundling Bay. Williams Island was more of a peninsula, whereas the South Island was a true island, connected to Williams by a bridge. To proceed with the construction of Privé, we would have to build a sidewalk of the South Island pursuant to Gary's previously approved deal with the city.

Gary went to the Aventura commissioners to vet everything. Commissioners reminded Gary of the condition precedent that if we were to start putting in our foundation, and particularly if we were going to develop Privé as something other than single-family homes, we would need to build a second sidewalk (a "second means of pedestrian egress," in formal parlance) on the South Island to prevent congestion. In essence, the city of Aventura had agreed to grant us permits to build our foundation, but only if we first completed construction of this new sidewalk. To do that, we needed to pull permits to build the sidewalk and see it through; the only catch was that the sidewalk would have to be built across land that was privately owned by South Island homeowners.

Gary's family had established vested rights on this land in Aventura, which included an easement over the part in question on the South Island. It was part of Gary's typically thoughtful and meticulous planning many years prior. He had known that one day, he would likely build on the North Island or sell to someone who would and that he needed to prepare for when that day came. To be ready, he mapped out the homes on his plat but also made sure he had a utility easement to put in a sidewalk. Even if his right to build that sidewalk on someone else's property wasn't exactly leaping off the page, the language supporting that argument was there all the same. With my background in law, I thought the situation seemed convoluted but tenable—but you learn in litigation that even the best positions or arguments can have equally convincing counter positions, even if they are legally illegitimate.

Gary explained to us that no matter how complex the legal claims might be, the sidewalk issue was a winnable fight —but perhaps not with the attorneys we had hired.

"We need to change our representation," Gary said. "The guys we have are good, but I'm not sure they have the grit we need to see this through to the end. We're going to need bulldogs." After hearing him explain, I couldn't have agreed more.

"These incumbents are good, but they're not the right fit for this," I said. "I want to bring in tough, aggressive counsel for this. We need an old-fashioned, New York-style fight here." After discussing it, we all agreed to go in a different direction. We hired Waldman Barnett, with a team led by Glen Waldman, who immediately began to clear a path, stand by our side and fight as fiercely as we needed.

We went to court again to show our permits and demonstrate that we were allowed to put a sidewalk in—and the South Island filed an Order to Show Cause against us (one of many over the course of the battle). It meant we had a temporary injunction that barred us from building our sidewalk— which in effect, meant derailing our entire project. It had been a huge blow; there was a lot of money on the line, but we were completely stuck. We knew we would have to appeal in the 3rd District Court of Appeals, but they were under no obligation to hear our case. At any rate, we got on their calendar all the same for a hearing 60 days out.

Incredibly enough, the court did hear our case—and they

gave us their approval that we had the legal right to build! After bouncing from circuit court to appeals court and back to circuit again, we pulled our permits and were ready to begin building—which we started doing immediately, now with both Williams Island and the South Island on a joint lawsuit against us. But they weren't done fighting. Despite the stress of the situation, I had to see the humor in it: one tiny stretch of sidewalk stood between us and the completion of a half-billion-dollar project.

With a legal path ostensibly cleared for us, the first step was to pour the concrete for the curb in place; it was made of brick pavers, so the curb would hold everything in. Though we had the right to build, the South Island homeowners brought out their heavy artillery to slow us down, parking an entire line of SUVs on the strip of land we intended to build on and having their nannies sit on the hoods. The idea was because the nannies were on the cars, we couldn't tow them out of there. To counter that, we had to hire an army of tow trucks on scene and play chicken with the homeowners. Whenever someone got off an SUV to go to the bathroom, we would send in our tow truck to haul it out. One woman in particular sat in the mud angrily and refused to move. When I went up to try and speak with her, she wouldn't listen and instead flipped me off (I was reminded of a line from *The Breakfast Club*: "Oh. Obscene finger gestures from such a pristine girl.").

Step by step over that summer in 2014, we installed all the sidewalk lining the fronts of the first 12 homes, with only three left to go. On what was supposed to be our final day finishing the sidewalk, Charlie was supervising the project while Gary and I were meeting with lawyers. Partway through the meeting, we got a call from Charlie.

"They drove over it!" he screamed into the phone.

"Charlie, calm down," Gary said. "They drove over what?"

"The curb!" Charlie replied. "They drove over the fucking curb!"

As he explained, even though we'd finally been allowed by the city and everyone else to keep building our sidewalk, it didn't matter. One of the homeowners living in front of the end of the island sidewalk hated what we were doing so much that she got in her SUV and drove over the curb while it was still setting, cracking it, deforming it and ultimately rendering it unusable. When we went to the site later on, it was clear from tire tracks that she'd tried to drive over much more of the rest of it as well. It was clear that a few of the homeowners were set against stopping our development by any means possible.

As Charlie explained, he went to check on the site and had caught a woman driving over our freshly poured sidewalk in her Porsche Cayenne. He pulled over, got out and asked her what the hell she thought she was doing.

"Fuck you, this is my property!" she replied to Charlie. "What the hell are *you* doing on my island? If you don't leave now, I'm going to call the cops." Charlie parked and told her to call the cops; he was not doing anything wrong. Sure enough, when the police came, the woman had been so belligerent that they arrested her! Later on, her husband had come to the scene in another car hoping to damage more of the sidewalk, and he was arrested too!

Soon after that, we were roped into another lawsuit—this

time alongside the arresting police officers and the city of Aventura itself. It was yet another front we would have to defend to bring our project to fruition.

Amid all the chaos, we were also fighting a PR war. There was a stream of negative coverage in local newspapers and blogs on the conflicts over Privé, and trying to keep buyers and agents in the units they'd pledged to buy was an uphill battle. Before long, the rhythm was that Gary would be on the phone with me, Greg and Charlie at odd hours of morning and night every other day. On top of that, we were constantly in and out of court and bouncing between court and the job site, managing the expectations of investors who were worried their money was in jeopardy and managing the sales team that there would actually be a product to sell at the end of the process.

"This project is really starting to grind us all down," I told Greg and Charlie one day.

"You know what I'm going to say, right?" Charlie asked.

"This is the one that's going to put us on the map?"

"That's right." What he and I both agreed on was that no matter how hard the project was, it was something that would 100x our brand, much like the joint venture with MSD had. If we could see this project through, we would compound our returns, invigorate ourselves and earn an even bigger name. Aside from all that, though, I had to appreciate his sense of humor—why couldn't we add some levity to the situation? On top of the risk of losing everything BH3 had worked for in this battle, there was the bigger risk of losing the purpose of it all: to have fun, build something that would last a lifetime and expand life's possibilities all at once. I decided that for the rest of the project, I would try to bring some of that positive energy back. And it would start in the PR war.

I realized we could punch back on the negative newspapers and magazine stories if we got creative. One of the first things was to helpfully provide some public information—namely, the mugshots of the people who had destroyed our sidewalk—to show how insane the South Island homeowners had gotten. Soon after, we were back in court again, with Williams Island and the South Island arguing against us.

"Your Honor," their representation said, "the developers are beginning the construction on the foundation, but the sidewalk is still incomplete!"

Of course, we immediately countered that the sidewalk had been complete until two homeowners had taken it on themselves to destroy it. Unfortunately, our opponents had a very nimble attorney countering our lawyers, so it was clear this part of the battle would drag on as well. If we were going to fight forever, I figured, we could at least keep adding fuel to the fire.

Because we owned the North Island, we were allowed to use the land for various purposes even if our actual building of the condos was taking forever. Why couldn't we use it for events before the building was done? And more specifically, events that would give back to the community and irritate the neighbors to no end all in one fell swoop? With that in mind, I went to the city of Aventura and attempted to pull permits to hold a special event. We (or I) decided that we would throw a benefit for indigent kids in the area on the North Island and that we would provide all the food and security for it. For security, I thought I could hire a host of local biker gangs to watch over everything—why not? I was in the process of getting everything approved when I got a call from Gary.

"Daniel, are you kidding me?" he yelled into the phone. "What are you trying to do on the North Island?"

The way we'd structured our deal was that as owner of the property trust, Gary was the proper owner of the North Island; BH3 had optioned it from him rather than bought it outright. So the city had given Gary a call that I'd filed and signed for a special event permit for him to approve.

"I appreciate your efforts on this project," he said, trying to hold back laughter, "but you've got to tone it down. The city is never going to approve our project with stunts like this." I agreed to shut it down, but I think my rebellious streak may have inspired Gary as well.

As the litigation dragged on, we kept chipping away at building our condos and maintaining our relationships with buyers and brokers. Behind the scenes, we were constantly trying to settle so the lawsuits would stop and we could proceed like we were allowed to. At every turn, there was a great deal of dramatic tension between all parties involved. Aside from constantly being on phone calls, we were in and out of engagements day and night, at all hours and often on weekends. We offered the South Island homeowners $35 million to stop fighting with us, but they refused. Later, we countersued Williams Island over an obscure clause in their title policies across all 2,500 units and 13 buildings that strengthened our own case. As it turned out, there was a restrictive covenant in the title that prevented them from suing or trying to prevent any development on the island—so they were effectively in breach of contract. As one final creative push, Gary had his own idea of how he would monetize the island without developing and get around the naysayers all at once.

In court, the residents on South Island and Williams Island were constantly arguing that we only had zoning for single-family homes—not for luxury condominiums (not strictly true, but that was their argument). Gary was always replying that the zoning didn't matter because of his vested rights—those rights were underneath everything and gave him leeway to develop the island as he saw fit. Still, the back and forth had given him an idea: if the other residents wanted to stop us from building, what if we didn't have to build at all? With that, Gary went to an architect and drew up plans for a trailer park.

The trick of it was to get around the local zoning restrictions, which Gary did as creatively as possible. He reached out to a trailer park company in Lake City, Florida, and used Type-D trailers. Those trailers had special approvals from FEMA and were allowed to be brought in and out of an area, circumventing whatever local zoning laws existed. Because of that, the city of Aventura had no control over stopping the trailers from coming in. Sure enough, Gary took his plans to the city with drawings for site approval. The city manager was there, and he sat through the entire presentation fuming. Finally, at the end of it, the city manager asked what the development would be called.

"Happy Acres of Aventura," Gary said proudly. The city manager's head was about to explode! A moment later, he turned to his attorney.

"Look through the local codes and find a way that we can stop him," he said. At that, Gary's attorney spoke up immediately.

"You can look through the codes, but there's nothing in them that can stop him," the attorney said, "and furthermore, that comment alone is actionable, and we can take you to court for it."

It finally looked like we were getting the upper hand: we would be profiting off the North Island no matter what the locals had to say about it. Of course, it was much more in the city's interest to not have a trailer park in the middle of a bunch of high-rise luxury developments. Sure enough, things started to turn after that in short order.

While we still had ongoing litigation to fend off, we successfully finished our sidewalk, allowing us to keep pushing forward. After more back and forth, we secured the permits to build our foundation and started on that. Slowly but surely, we managed to erect our towers and top them on the North Island. It had taken 27 months from when we broke ground, but the project was well on its way to completion despite all obstacles. Because it was all built, there was little reason to keep fighting anymore—even though the homeowners all still seemed to want to. Finally, in March 2018—five years after the litigation had begun—the judge ruled in our favor against Williams Island. The ruling stated that the association had breached their agreement from 1982, barring island residents from suing Gary over future development. As a result, the judge and jury awarded us $26 million plus several million in interest from the Williams Island property owners. The irony, of course, is that we'd offered to pay the South Island nearly the same amount just to stop fighting us, and they'd refused!

After the case ended, we settled with Williams Island for a confidential sum, but I can say it was in excess of $21 million, and it came with the additional conditions that the case couldn't be appealed again in the future and that we would receive payment within 30 days. It felt like it had taken years off our lives to get to a settlement, but it was a truly remarkable achievement—in fact, it remains the largest settlement paid out to developers in South Florida to date.

Aside from the legal battles, keeping our investors, construction crews and sales team on track was an art all to itself. In the latter case, we brought Michael Neumann out of retirement, with whom we had worked on Trump Hollywood. On Trump Hollywood, Michael had proved himself as the best condo salesman in South Florida by helping us sell out our project after we had hired and fired three other sales managers. Because Privé was so special to us, we knew we needed the best of the best.

But amidst all the mayhem of keeping so many different teams in balance, one of the most invigorating aspects of Privé was the interior design and art curation process, the latter of which I helped spearhead. It was a way for me to find what I called "distraction through abstraction." Because Privé had 70,000 square feet of common area, we had to buy several million dollars' worth of art to fill it. It meant that between court battles and putting out other fires, I was flying to places like Atlanta and California to meet different artists and see their studios.

With the help of my friends Kipton Cronkite and Julia Chi, I was introduced to artists, including David Paul Kay. David had grown up in war-torn Georgia and had a complicated youth, the energy of which manifested in his art. After meeting him and connecting with his story, we commissioned him to do a series of giant mixed-media canvases that were black and white and drawn primarily in Sharpie, staggering in their complexity and scale. I also met Domingo Zapata through my dear friend James, a Spanish artist whose neo-expressionist and graffiti-like color techniques were captivating. He was a well-known world-traveled artist spending some of his time in South Florida as well, and after we hit it off, we commissioned him to do a dozen pieces for Privé.

Spending time with artists and filling the finished building with color and texture was so inspiring that it made all the struggles worth it—it was truly the ultimate merger of art and commerce and felt like the culmination of so many different aspects of my life up to that point. Although the artists and sculptors were inspiring in their own way, meeting Ross Bleckner was an experience that taught me an important lesson.

In the process of vetting different artists, I saw a few things that didn't inspire me before flying up to Ross's studio in Manhattan to see his work. Right away, it was clear he was an incredibly prolific painter and a deep thinker. Walking around his studio, there were 10 massive canvases, each one abstract, emotional and intense in its own unique way. It was clear that this space was completely infused with Ross's personality, and I was still getting my bearings in it.

As we walked through together, I noticed a table with many standard small 8.5" x 11" canvases on it. Unlike some of the other huge canvases, each of these small paintings looked quite similar; all of them had the same flower painted again and again. As he caught me looking at the table, he smiled.

"Do you know what it is?" he asked me, gesturing to one of the paintings.

"It's the same flower painted over and over again, right?" I replied.

"Years ago, I met this artist who was in the process of painting a poppy flower," Ross said. "I was taken by his style and approach, and ever since then, I come in early before I get started, and I paint the same flower. Each time, the painting is a little different, but this is how I get ready to paint. This is how I prime my mind and my hands."

In that moment, everything in the studio took on new significance. Compared to some of the more eye-catching, big canvases in his studio, these smaller poppies were easy to overlook—but to Ross, they were the keystone of his process. As Privé was coming to an end, it was easy to marvel at its scale and how perfectly so many things needed to line up for it to happen—all despite enormous pushback. The result was what I considered an artistic masterpiece of real estate, but it had not popped into the world fully formed; it had been the product of many different people's brushstrokes, compounded over decades.

I knew there would always be more real estate deals and new challenges to take on, but there was a sense of finality that came with Privé. How would we top ourselves here? When would we get the chance to do something this amazing again? Looking at Ross's poppies, I knew the answer was right in front of me. You don't get to paint the next masterpiece all at once, but the next one would come organically if I never forgot about priming. Greg, Charlie, Gary and I had pushed as hard as we could for years to see Privé to completion, just like it had taken Ross his entire life, in a sense, to create the best of his works in the present.

After seeing his studio, I insisted that Ross fly down to Miami to see the unfinished project at Privé. Upon seeing it, it was clear to him what I was trying to do and that we could work together. I commissioned him as well, and as a kind gesture amongst friends, he gave me one of his prized poppy paintings.

To this day, I smile when I look at it. It showed that no matter the scale of my accomplishments, there was always still more to do—more relationships to build and more positive ripple effects to initiate. Masterpieces may have been remarkably rare, but to even have the chance of painting one, you had to pick up the brush every day. It was what had made Privé and BH3 possible in the first place, and I had no intention of changing my plans.

EPILOGUE

On our 10th wedding anniversary, Rachel and I went to Florence, Italy. After reading for a few hours while she got ready, we left the hotel and arrived at a beautiful restaurant called Buca Mario to eat amazing seafood and drink red wine. The entire time, I kept looking up at a painting on the wall above us. The picture showed two men playing poker across a table from one another. One of the poker players was in casual clothes and had a cigarette in his mouth, and across from him were his opponent in a tattered suit jacket and a third man watching the game. All three had the most vivid facial expressions.

The closer I looked, it was obvious one was the victor, one was clearly losing and the third was scowling as if to say, "You idiot! How many times are you going to suffer like this?" I couldn't take my eyes off it.

Eventually, I had the waiter call the manager over to the table (neither of whom spoke English).

"I want to know about this painting," I said, pulling in

another guest to help me translate what I was saying. After some back and forth, the manager told me that it had been on the wall for 20 years.

"Listen, I don't want to be disrespectful," I said, "but would you be interested in selling it by any chance?" A few moments later, the waiter and the manager were talking to the restaurant's real owners—an older husband and wife. Again, after some belabored back and forth and makeshift translating, the staff pulled the painting off the wall. I put my credit card down and paid for the meal, plus an additional $10,000 for the painting on the spot.

The waitstaff took it back to the kitchen and wrapped it in butcher paper, and we left the restaurant with it under my arm. Still, I hadn't realized the complex situation I'd just gotten Rachel and me into on our anniversary. Soon enough, it was clear, getting the painting back through customs would be very difficult—particularly because I wanted to keep the frame. The result was that I schlepped it around Italy with me everywhere I went—at beaches on the Amalfi Coast, at a beautiful vineyard in Tuscany. While Rachel sipped wine and took in the scenery, I would sneak away for a few minutes at a time to make phone calls and conjure up a way to get this undervalued gem back to Florida with me in one piece.

Finally, I went to the concierge at our hotel and asked for a wrench and some pliers. After dinner one night, I pulled the frame apart delicately with the tools, keeping each piece of the frame intact and throwing away the dusty old glass. Before leaving the country, I had the painting rolled in a tube and the framing packaged and shipped separately. Back stateside a few weeks later, the pieces arrived, and I sent them out to be reconstructed and the painting to be cleaned and restored.

Finally, the finished piece was mounted on our wall at home, and I couldn't have been happier—the resulting work had restored all the beautiful details I knew were there under the dust that I'd sensed that day in the restaurant. Rachel's reaction was a little more bemused.

"So, do you really think it was worth all the hassle?" she asked me, raising an eyebrow. I just smiled. She already knew that any trip with me was bound to become an adventure.

THE INFINITE CANVAS

Years after Harry and I had begun our business doing note deals in New York, we happened to find ourselves in Israel together, walking down Sheinkin Street in downtown Tel Aviv. Harry was showing me his grandmother's apartment and explaining how she used to watch his dad from the balcony while he sold sabras in the streets to people walking back and forth across from the Shuk HaCarmel. I had heard the story before but was shocked after he pointed out exactly which apartment his grandmother had lived in.

"Harry, I knew our parents knew each other growing up in Israel," I said, "but did you know that my mother's childhood home was down the road on the exact same street where your father grew up?" Sure enough, we walked a couple of blocks more, and I pointed out 23 Sheinkin Street, where my mother had lived as a girl in the 1940s and '50s. My mom had told me that when she was young, that one-bedroom apartment had housed seven people spanning three generations. Seeing it in person, it was hard to imagine how they managed.

Being with my dear friend in the exact spot in the Holy Land where our parents had been raised was intense. Our parents had lived virtually next door to each other decades before separately moving across the world, to the same country, state and town and sending their kids to the same private school where their children met and formed a lifelong connection. From those humble beginnings, Harry and I are in our fourth decade of friendship and second decade of business partnership. It's an ongoing story, but the seeds of it have been germinating in the Holy Land for decades, all on the same street.

It reminds me of what I see when I look out my window at my apartment in Privé today—a gorgeous view of Dumfoundling Bay, the Florida sunshine, the vibrant culture of Miami all around me and across the way, my future mother-in-law's balcony, which I had stood on a decade before while staring at a blank island and imagining all the possibilities. It's enough to inspire anyone to start reminiscing, so please allow me a brief indulgence.

Since its inception, BH3 has expanded its horizons. Today, it is a company with multiple investment vehicles, namely a debt opportunity fund to invest in distressed debt and do bridge loans, a select development business and an "opportunistic investment bucket"—the latter has included buying an old, abandoned warehouse that we turned into offices with art and murals on the facade, structured as a tax exemption opportunity zone deal. Through all these evolutions, our core DNA has remained the same, as has our sense of humility.

As I think of all that while looking out my window at a gorgeous view, I always remember that the so-called "top" isn't where I feel most at home. I'm most at home when I'm in my trailer on the water in Delray Beach. When Kurt brought his daughter with him to see it, he was a little confused. His exact words were: "This place is a shithole, but I get it." Some people get it; some don't.

I love the so-called finer things in life, but they're not the most important things to me. Early in my career, the choices were more about achieving financial gain or advancing in some way—and when those things had not yet materialized, the journey was not always fun. On the other side of it all, it was easy to be more optimistic and say that it has always been about the struggle, enjoying the journey and building relationships. Kurt's comment about my trailer is a good indication of that, and it has resonated with me since that day.

My friend Eric Newman's father was a rough guy from Brownsville, Brooklyn, who gave me some advice a long time ago to roughly the same effect: "You're lucky in life if you have one true friend." It sounds cynical, but when you think about it, it's not an unreasonable comment. There are plenty of people out there who don't have friends—at least, no real ones they could call brothers and sisters. The art of life is about finding those connections and dedicating the requisite sincerity and intention to each one. It means treating your personal relationships and business endeavors with the same dedication and seriousness and building something beautiful out of both. It's an approach of looking for the deeper narratives behind things, and it's one I've kept in mind when collecting art as well.

The connection between art and real estate is both

obvious and nuanced. On a basic level, there's artistry that goes into making a building look beautiful and in constructing or reconstructing a deal. Looking more deeply, when it comes to bringing community back to developed neighborhoods—places like the Village, Alphabet City, Wynwood and South Beach—the way they came back to life in the first place was through art. Each of the pioneers who reinvented those neighborhoods embraced and invited artists, photographers, fashion designers and other creatives to start conversations that reverberate to this day. That kind of public artwork sends a signal to young creatives like painters, fashion designers, photographers that the area is a safe place for them to express themselves. That's where it starts—that heartbeat of creativity. People follow the art.

As I've gotten older, I've learned more about spirituality, life and family. To some extent, I've calmed down and have hopefully become a bit wiser, but the truth is, I don't feel all that different from the restless Long Island teenager who had a proclivity for fist fighting. Ultimately, I try to approach life openly and with a mind for collaboration and "being a mensch," but I'm never afraid to fight—it's just the scope of the fights and the size of the opponents that have changed.

Even after you've raised a family, built a business and found what many people would call success, there aren't many moments where everything clicks into place, and you can see the scale of everything you've accomplished. The scale of what BH3 has done doesn't even hit me most of the time, even though many of our buildings are singular and visually special. It usually only happens when I'm talking with close friends, reflecting with Greg or when I walk through some of our projects.

On a building like Privé, for example, the concrete foundation must be strong enough to support 160 condominiums —hundreds of thousands of pounds of glass and concrete. Meanwhile, the building does not just rest on the surface of the island; it is set on over 2,400 auger piles, each one driven approximately 72 feet into the ground. The building's two-level garage rests on top of those, and the whole thing rises some 201 feet into the air, able to resist windstorms and all of nature's elements. Architecturally speaking, the building's height wouldn't be possible without that foundational depth undergirding it. All that combined effort results in a structure you can see from outer space.

When I'm in the empty garage and I consider all the people and all the now invisible construction that went into it, I feel like I'm in the guts of some enormous machine. As I talk to the security guards, management, and the valets and owners streaming in and out of the buildings in the morning, it forces me to realize how big the world is and how many people it takes to achieve great accomplishments. It reminds me of what Dan Sullivan asks in his Strategic Coach programs: "To whom do you want to be a hero?" I only want to be a hero to my kids, my friends and my partners. To do that, I tell myself how crucial it is to remain humble and well-purposed and that my life would not be possible without the help of countless others and the universe's good fortune, both earned and unearned. All of it is a privilege for which I will be forever grateful.

Aside from my devotion to my daughters, the most fascinating part of my life right now is rediscovering my roots in a different way: by tapping into creativity and art. In all our new buildings, I look for opportunities to include paintings in the lobby and artistic touches throughout. I've also become more involved in commissioning murals that will brighten up people's lives through Paint the City. Of course, writing this book has also put me back in touch with the kid who wanted to write the next Great American Novel and has helped me see my own journey again through younger eyes.

No matter how life develops next, I know new spaces and places are always opening for my loved ones and me. Even if those new opportunities lead to mistakes or imperfections, I remind myself that they are all a part of the fabric and that they may, in turn, lead to even better opportunities. Everything is imperfect, but life is an infinite canvas we're all painting on, and it keeps unrolling no matter which direction we turn. There's no end to it—all we can do is splash new colors down and watch them compound. Once you stop yourself from always thinking about the end of things, you give yourself permission to get lost in the process, which is where the joy lies.

Part of why "getting on the map" is so funny to Greg and me as a business concept is that there's a level of irony to it. The truth is you are always on the map; you just have to learn to appreciate where you're standing. When you do, you find that every small moment with people and every tiny step forward matters tremendously. With the right perspective, the idea of achieving wealth or status or some other far-off dream in the future melts away because you realize that what's happening *right now* with the people you care about around you is the most important thing of all. It's actually the only thing that exists.

Ultimately, I've found that this mantra is relatively all-purpose when it comes to life and relationships, but only if you apply it the right way. Whether you feel you have it all already or you're still on your journey, whether things are going smoothly or you're being hit with so much adversity that it seems like everything is going to fall apart, you always have the choice to take a breath and greet the world with a smile. *This is the one that will put us on the map. This is the one.*

ACKNOWLEDGMENTS

To my daughters—You are my everything, and you both have the ingredients to be and become anything you desire. Don't squander it, and don't listen to anyone who says you cannot because you can. Marry your dreams with your reality, but don't be fooled—it requires work and dedication. I love you so much and encourage you to carve your own path, write your own stories, break boundaries, enjoy life, be in good company or no company at all, be proud of your heritage and always find the gold lining in all things because I assure you, it is there.

To my parents—What can I say, for never having read a book on raising kids or the master guide to having a family (which does not exist), you have and continue to do great. Ours was a quirky household with our own special sauce—immigrant's delight— from the battles over the thermostat to the garage sale adventures. It's been a colorful journey, and you have unequivocally helped make it that way. Your strength through the inconceivable has always been a bold reminder of the import of grit and just an absolute inspiration. Your indulgence in all my jokes, so many of which you have been the subject of, is always appreciated.

To my sister Alisa—I love you, appreciate you and appreciate you staying close to the hoop when it may not have always felt particularly good. You have always encouraged me, been there when I needed you, and I am so proud of you and your accomplishments. Stay bold.

To my sister Tammy—I miss you and think of you often.

To my dear friends and brothers—I am in awe of you. You bring the brightest colors to my life's canvas. You inspire me, you encourage me, you humble me, you teach me, you make me better, and overall, just make my life entirely more fulfilling. I cannot imagine the journey, the lessons, the celebrations and the struggles without you. Greg, Ari, Kurt, David, Harry, Yaniv, Steve, Scott, Eric, Gary, Eddie, Fares, David, David, Joel, Dan, Parviz, Martin, Lenny, Jim, Michael, Simon, Barry, Ilya and numerous others.

To all the dads who have taken the time over the years and with whom I have built bonds, and all the moms who have nurtured my friends and always welcomed me into their homes with open arms—I can't thank you enough.

To the entire Launch Pad team—Thank you for your collaboration. In particular, Anna—I'm grateful for your enthusiasm, feedback and guidance. Your impact in all that you do has massive ripple effects. Ryan—Your collaboration, your ear, our conversations are all deeply appreciated, and I look forward to continuing the conversation for years to come.

To Joe Polish—Thank you for connecting me with Launch Pad (and inspiring me to wear my shit proudly).

To Dan Sullivan and the Strategic Coach members I have exchanged so many notes with over the years—It has been energizing and a giant mirror for illuminating in me how much more capacity I have to grow and contribute.

To myself—Go easy, let go of the self-criticism, be present, be forgiving, be inspired, inspire, create, love, dream, imagine, leap often and don't get caught in the bullshit.

ABOUT THE AUTHOR

Daniel Lebensohn is a founder, co-CEO and board member of BH3, a real estate investment firm with properties in New York and Florida. Before founding BH3, Lebensohn practiced law in New York City for more than 12 years while managing his own commercial and multifamily properties. A father of two, Lebensohn continues to nurture his real estate business and artistic collaborations. He is at work on his second book, *ROSE: Return on Sweat Equity*.